A READER FOR THE
POLITICALLY INCORRECT

A READER FOR THE
POLITICALLY INCORRECT

GEORGE ZILBERGELD

Westport, Connecticut
London

Library of Congress Cataloging-in-Publication Data

Zilbergeld, George, 1941–
    A reader for the politically incorrect/by George Zilbergeld.
        p. cm.
    Includes bibliographical references and index.
    ISBN 0-275-97762-5 (alk. paper)—ISBN 0-275-97763-3 (pbk.: alk. paper)
    1. Political correctness. I. Title.
    HM1216.Z55 2003
    306—dc22   2003057987

British Library Cataloguing in Publication Data is available.

Library of Congress Catalog Card Number: 2003057987
ISBN: 0-275-97762-5
        0-275-97763-3 (paperback)

First published in 2003

Praeger Publishers, 88 Post Road West, Westport, CT 06881
An imprint of Greenwood Publishing Group, Inc.
www.praeger.com

Printed in the United States of America

The paper used in this book complies with the
Permanent Paper Standard issued by the National
Information Standards Organization (Z39.48–1984).

10 9 8 7 6 5 4 3 2 1

Copyright Acknowledgments

Contents

Introduction

The term "politically correct" (PC) was first used by supporters of the Communist Revolution in Russia. They decided that it would be politically incorrect to speak up about the mass murders being committed by the revolutionary government, since doing so would give comfort to the enemies of the revolution. To be politically correct was to support the promised goal of absolute equality, even if the means included mass murder.

Today being politically correct does not include tolerating mass murder, but it does include the same willingness to destroy Western civilization in order to build a more perfect world. It also involves a similar belief in the need for a self-elected elite vanguard to lead the way to this perfect future.

Current political correctness is based on the belief that liberty, until now the prime value of Western civilization, must be supplanted by a new prime value—equality. Unlike the old revolutionaries, the new politically correct revolutionaries no longer believe that the old strategy of a violent overthrow of our government is necessary. The PC much prefer a march through the institutions of the judiciary, the bureaucracy, and, above all, the educational system. The PC believe that they will soon dominate enough of the country to complete the changes needed to create a new and better world.

The PC establishment has created an atmosphere on many college campuses and elsewhere that squelches debate on many important academic and political topics. This viewpoint has completely altered the nature of college education, making most colleges separate communities that view themselves as morally superior and as having a right to be paid to lecture other folks on how they should live their lives. Even though the PC are a minority on college campuses, their intensity, passion, and willingness to be confrontational have won them victory after victory. Most university professors are liberal democrats who still honor ideas like freedom of speech, but so far they have proven to be no match for the PC, who have shown a religious devotion to their cause. The leaders of the PC movement believe that they are anointed as doctors working on the soul of mankind for the eventual betterment of all.

These true believers are certain that they have a path that will bring salvation, peace, and harmony to the United States and, eventually, the whole human race. They promise that while individual rights may have to be reduced or eliminated for a while, it will be worthwhile. At times they say that these rights are just an illusion, which you will understand as soon as they "raise your consciousness." Thus they often speak of their support for "real" freedom and "real" democracy. Their "real" democracy is never in existence now, but will come into being, they say, after they are in charge. After the revolution, we will enjoy "real" freedom. Our new rights will include an extraordinary form of equality that will take no notice of any secondary characteristics, such as race, ethnicity, gender, or any other arbitrary characteristics of human beings. None of the seemingly random aspects of life, such as looks, parents, physical ability, place of birth, or socioeconomic standing will have any impact on how we are treated.

The PC view teaches that the Western world, America, white people, men, and heterosexuals are the source of evil and the cause of the flawed world we live in. This reflects the Marxist view of the world, except that other "marginalized" groups, including "people of color," women, and homosexuals join the workers as part of the larger group that will be saved while saving the world. The PC focus on the real and imagined failures and deficiencies of America and the West, especially racism and sexism, to the exclusion of their virtues and accomplishments. The PC seek to "deconstruct" or "decenter" the West, America, white people, men, and heterosexuals. Their jargon is based on the belief that the power of these groups is based solely on exploiting others. They argue that the power of the dominant groups (usually white men) determines what we think is true or real. They frequently reject the idea of an objective reality in history, morality, or even science. Reality, they believe, is just something built or constructed by those in power. Many among the PC view all or most of reality itself as a social construct. A powerful current within PC maintains that morality is just a construction that supports the claims of white people, men, and the West. This latter argument has become less politically effective since September 11, now that many Americans have decided that they darn well know what is evil and are ready to fight against it. Their intention is to destroy or greatly reduce the power of the now dominant groups, including the entire Western world, after which a utopian world free of any oppression will replace it.

Their first step is to make the majority lose confidence in their values, institutions, societal arrangements, and government, at which point people will
see the wisdom of letting the PC create a new society that will have none of
the failings of the old. The PC are obsessed with the defects of the middle
class, suburban life, the military, white people, men, and heterosexuals,
because they believe that the dominance of these groups prevents a new and
better world from coming into existence.

Any group that represents the West is also considered to be part of the
structure that must be attacked and whose flaws must be front-and-center
in any analysis. This explains the incessant attacks on, for example, the U.S.
military. It explains the PC's constant attacks on Israel, which is viewed as
part of the West. This also explains why they are not filled with joy at the
thought of the United States winning a rapid and complete victory in
Afghanistan. This is why they are constantly critical of the war effort, noting things that will or can go wrong, and constantly downplaying the sins
of our enemies. The now nervous PC repeatedly suggest that while it may
be good to pursue the terrorists, we should rely on the United Nations,
we will get bogged down, we have the wrong allies, we are moving too fast
or too slow, are causing too many civilian casualties, and so on. Almost
any criticism will do. The idea of the United States triumphant fills them
with despair.

This book was created with the belief that two of the basic goals of education are the empowerment of the students and citizens. I think that an
important element of empowerment consists of providing students with the
opportunity to hear all sides of an issue. The politically correct professors
say that this is not necessary because the outside world presents the other
more traditional view. I think that they are wrong and that most of the
major media support the politically correct view. But the important point is
that if universities are to be fortresses of liberty, they must support the pre-
sentation of different views; and if they are to be acting in partnership with
a scientific age, they must support the openness, the belief in an objective
reality, and the reliance on facts that are the hallmarks of science.

To say that only one view is to be presented is to take the attitude of a
church. Indeed, many would say that being politically correct is a religion
for many of the professors and their off-campus followers. Being politically
correct seems to be a good fit for those who have a religious sensibility and
seem to need a worldview that tells them what the ultimate goal of life is
and how to judge themselves and others. Political correctness seems to fill
the religious needs of those who wish to believe but have trouble believing
in a god, except perhaps themselves collectively. Certainly on most campuses,
when discussing any subject that is of interest to the politically correct, you
are more likely to hear "shh" or "if you believe, think, say that, you are
(racist, sexist, homophobic, insensitive etc.), and you will be cast into the
outer darkness of the unenlightened," than you are to hear words that

should characterize a university, such as, "You got any proof for that, Bud?" The result on many campuses is that the politically correct have constituted themselves as a church of the perpetually self-righteous. This is definitely the church before the reformation. The intensity of their belief matches their certainty. When this is combined with the fact that students are so dependent on their professors, you have the making of a strange new totalitarian culture. This may be comforting for the true believers, but not for most students and not for those who are concerned for the future of a truly free society.

For twenty-five years, I have been a professor who has watched as the politically correct have gained a chokehold on campus after campus. They have used their power to control more and more policies on campus. They now have great control over freshman orientation, campus speakers, course offerings, general education requirements, course material, and hiring.

Still, I can't help thinking that the control of schools by the politically correct is the world's largest "the emperor has no clothes" situation. The politically correct professors are still afraid that the public will find out what is happening. They still feel the need to go into a frenzy of spin whenever examples of their political correctness become public. They are wise to do so. They know that they are not suited to work outside of the university and thus are dependent on the public they despise. Often public exposure leads to a change in policy. For example, consider the method used at Cornell to insure that all student dormitory managers were politically correct. Candidates for these positions were shown a pornographic film featuring homosexuals. They were observed and videotaped while watching the film. Students who seemed to show a dislike of such activity were interrogated, shown the videotape of their reactions, and removed unless they could provide a satisfactory reason for not enjoying the film. When this was made public, the showing of the film was promptly dropped.

Ultimately this is a weak position. Most students still believe that this is a good country and that the West is the only place they ever wish to live. Every semester I ask my students where they would live if they couldn't live in the United States. For twenty-five years, over 95 percent of every class has chosen a country that is part of Western civilization. The most popular speakers I invite to my classes are combat veterans. Poll-after-poll reveals that most Americans believe that this is fundamentally a good country. The only exception to the more positive view is shown in polls of Ivy League colleges. It is true that the graduates of these schools play a particularly important role in the least democratic institutions of our society, such as the colleges, bureaucracies, and the judiciary. Still, the overwhelming majority of students and citizens disagree with this elite and believe in the values of Western civilization and the goodness of America. I believe that Freud was right when he said that the voice of reason is small, but it is relentless and often wins in the long run. In a country that I believe is not inherently racist, sexist, or unenlightened, and certainly not of worse character than most professors, I think that the voice of reason will prevail.

I remember a poem about a man whose grandfather came to America to become his own king. This is a book for people who are not worried that they will be cast into the outer darkness if they disagree with the politically correct of our times. As they say in the finest diners in America: enjoy.

Each of the chapters of this book deals with an area that has been an important battlefield for the PC. The first chapter deals with the particularly important topic of the impact of political correctness on education, followed by chapters on the co-opting of the environmental movement by the PC, on affirmative action (an area in which the undemocratic techniques of the PC are particularly clear), and on attitudes toward war and veterans. The book concludes with a chapter on the conflict between the PC and their opponents, often referred to as the culture wars.

I place particular emphasis on education because one cannot be a responsible citizen without a thorough knowledge of the civilization that created liberty and democracy and its successes as well as its failures. In addition, a politically correct education enforces habits that are not compatible with liberty and democracy. It closes off the asking of important questions and supports a view of the world in which people who disagree with you are enemies to be destroyed, instead of opponents who disagree on a particular issue, but whose rights must still be protected. The PC view eliminates the open university that supports an open society.

Political Correctness
and Education

This chapter explains the destructive impact that politically correct thinking has had on education. "Taking Offense" is the first account of the politically correct movement that appeared in a major national magazine. It suggests that the growing power of political correctness on college campuses may constitute a kind of "new McCarthyism," violating freedom of speech and smothering open discussion. Colleges in America have been the main source of PC thought and the first major institution conquered by the PC movement. Academia, especially in the humanities and social sciences, with particular emphasis in English and comparative literature, remains the heart of the PC movement. It supplies most of its ideology, energy, and power to indoctrinate young people and win recruits. Its impact on college campuses has been extraordinary.

"Thought Reform 101: The Orwellian implications of Today's College Orientation," by Alan Charles Kors, describes the aggressive indoctrination methods, sometimes reminiscent of the communist "self-criticism" sessions, which are used at many colleges today. Kors shows how the politically correct have managed to gain great power in the administration of numerous colleges, obtaining positions that enable them to indoctrinate students with PC views. The article by professor Kagan explains why we need to study Western civilization. The study of Western civilization is often reduced to a study of the evils of Western civilization or, whenever possible, it is eliminated as part of the mandatory curriculum. The PC attack Western civilization as part of their project to destroy support for the prime value of liberty and substitute equality, which they say will bring about a superior civilization that will amount to a paradise on earth. But without an education that allows us to appreciate the importance and fragility of liberty, we may be unable to maintain our democratic institutions. If the history of the twentieth century is any guide, having equality as the prime value of a society seems to result in no liberty and a great deal of slaughter.

Christina Sommers argues that the PC do not hesitate to bend facts if it helps them win public arguments. "Where the Boys Are" shows that a portion of the women's movement has gone beyond calling for equality in society and the classroom and seeks to eradicate many masculine characteristics in elementary school boys.

The PC do not hesitate to use their positions to insure that only those who agree with them are given influential positions. Some of these positions offered to students, such as resident assistant positions, are highly prized since they often provide free room and board. A pledge that potential student dormitory managers must sign before they can get the coveted positions is included here to illustrate the current power of the PC in controlling the staff positions, in this case the directors of dormitories. The excerpt from Paula Rothenberg's best-selling textbook makes the views of the PC explicit, something that is not always done in the classroom so as not to alarm the students. These views underlie nearly all the classroom analysis of the PC. These views may be softened from time-to-time, but they are always there.

"What is Lost With a Politically Correct Education," by George Zilbergeld summarizes the effects of a PC education and explains why students, parents, and citizens ought to be worried when the PC substitute indoctrination for education.

Reading 1
TAKING OFFENSE
Newsweek

Is this the new enlightenment on campus or the new McCarthyism?

Perhaps Nina Wu, a sophomore at the University of Connecticut, actually didn't like gays. More likely, she thought she was being funny when she allegedly put up a sign on the door to her dorm room listing "people who are shot on sight"—among them, "preppies," "bimbos," "men without chest hair," and "homos." No protests were heard from representatives of the first three categories, but UConn's gay community was more forthright in asserting its prerogatives. Wu was brought up on charges of violating the student-behavior code, which had recently been rewritten to prohibit "posting or advertising publicly offensive, indecent or abusive matter concerning persons . . . and making personal slurs or epithets based on race, sex, ethnic origin, disability, religion or sexual orientation." Found guilty last year in a campus administrative hearing, Wu was . . . What would you guess? Reprimanded? Ordered to write a letter of apology? No, Wu was ordered to move off campus and forbidden to set foot in any university dormitories or cafeterias. Only under pressure of a federal lawsuit did the university let her move back onto campus this year—and revise the Code of Student Conduct to make it conform to a higher code, the First Amendment.

There is an experiment of sorts taking place in American colleges. Or, more accurately, hundreds of experiments at different campuses, directed at changing the consciousness of this entire generation of university students. The goal is to eliminate prejudice, not just of the petty sort that shows up on sophomore dorm walls, but the grand prejudice that has ruled American universities since their founding: that the intellectual tradition of Western Europe occupies the central place in the history of civilization. In this context it would not be enough for a student to refrain from insulting homosexuals or other minorities. He or she would be expected to "affirm" their presence on campus and to study their literature and culture alongside that of Plato, Shakespeare, and Locke. This agenda is broadly shared by most organizations of minority students, feminists, and gays. It is also the program of a generation of campus radicals who grew up in the '60s and are now achieving positions of academic influence. If they no longer talk of taking to the streets, it is because they now are gaining access to the conventional weapons of campus politics: social pressure, academic perks (including tenure) and—when they have the administration on their side—outright coercion. There is no conspiracy at work here, just a creed, a set of beliefs and expressions, which students from places as diverse as Sarah Lawrence and San Francisco State recognize instantly as "PC"—politically correct. Plunk down a professor from Princeton, say, in the University of Wisconsin at Madison, show him a student in a tie-dyed T-shirt, with open-toed sandals and a grubby knapsack dangling a student-union-issue, environmentally sound, reusable red plastic cup, and he'll recognize the type instantly. It's "PC Person," an archetype that has now been certified in the official chronicles of American culture, the comic pages. Jeff Shesol, a student cartoonist at Brown, created him as an enforcer of radical cant, so sensitive to potential slights that he even knows the correct euphemism for 9-year-old "girls." He calls them "pre-women."

That is appalling, or would be if it were true. What happened to Nina Wu is in fact appalling, as the university itself seems to have admitted. But so was the incident that led UConn to prohibit "personal slurs" in the first place: a group of white students taunting and spitting at Asian-American students on their way to a dance. If women, gays and racial minorities are seeking special protections, it is because they have been the objects of special attacks. (According to sociologist Howard Ehrlich, each year one minority student in five experiences "ethnoviolent attack," including verbal assaults.) If African-Americans are challenging the primacy of Western civilization, it is because for centuries they were oppressed by it. The oppressed have no monopoly on truth. But surely they have earned the right to critique the society that enslaved them.

The content of PC is, in some respects, uncontroversial: who would *defend* racism? What is distressing is that at the university, of all places, tolerance has to be imposed rather than taught, and that "progress" so often is just the replacement of one repressive orthodoxy by another.

Shelf struggle: The march of PC across American campuses has hardly been unopposed. On the contrary, it has provoked the most extreme reaction, from heartfelt defenses of the First Amendment to the end-of-the-world angst of a Rabelais scholar whose subject has just been dropped from the freshman lit course in favor of Toni Morrison. Opponents of PC now have their own organization, the National Association of Scholars (based in Princeton, N.J.), "committed to rational discourse as the foundation of academic life." Mostly conservative foundations support it, but its 1,400 members include some prominent liberals such as Duke political scientist James David Barber, former chair of Amnesty International USA. Duke is a microcosm of the struggle over PC, which is being fought right down to the shelves in the campus bookstore, and not always entirely by rational discourse. Barber stalked into the political-science section one day last spring and turned on its spine every volume with "Marx" in its title—about one out of seven by his count, a lot more attention than he thought it warrants—and angrily demanded their removal. His attempt to organize an NAS chapter at Duke touched off a battle with the influential head of the English department, Stanley Fish, which was extreme even by academic standards of vitriol. Fish called NAS, and by implication its members, "racist, sexist, and homophobic." "That," notes one of Barber's allies, "is like calling someone a communist in the McCarthy years."

Opponents of PC see themselves as a beleaguered minority among barbarians who would ban Shakespeare because he didn't write in Swahili. Outnumbered they may be on some campuses, but they are also often the most senior and influential people on their faculties. "We know who's in," says Martin Kilson, a black professor of government at Harvard, "and it's not women or blacks. That's a damned lie!" And whenever the campus comes into conflict with the power structure of society, it's no contest.

Last week a bureaucrat in the Department of Education jeopardized decades of progress in affirmative action by threatening the loss of federal funds to universities that award scholarships specifically for minority students.

But where the PC reigns, one defies it at one's peril. That was the experience of Prof. Vincent Sarich of the University of California, Berkeley, when he wrote in the alumni magazine that the university's affirmative action program discriminated against white and Asian applicants. Seventy-five students marched into his anthropology class last month and drowned out his lecture with chants of "bullshit." His department began an investigation of his views and chancellor Chang-Lin Tien invited complaints from students about his lectures. Sarich was left in doubt whether he would be allowed to teach the introductory anthropology course he has taught off and on for twenty-three years.

Of course, Sarich was not entirely an innocent who blundered into the minefield of campus politics. He holds scientifically controversial views about the relationship of brain size to intelligence, which tends toward the politically unthinkable conclusion that some races could have a genetic edge in intellect. (He does not, however, bring these up in his introductory course.) As an anthropologist, Sarich knows exactly what happened to him: he stumbled on a taboo. "There are subjects you don't even talk or think about," Sarich says: among them, "race, gender [and] homosexuality."

Rude comments: It is not just wildly unfashionable views like Sarich's that are taboo. Students censor even the most ordinary of opinions. Nicole Stelle, a Stanford junior, spent this past semester working and studying in Washington, and found it easier to be a liberal in Republican Sen. Robert Dole's office than a conservative at Stanford. "If I was at lunch [in the dorm] and we started talking about something like civil rights, I'd get up and leave . . . I knew they didn't want to hear what I had to say."

PC is, strictly speaking, a totalitarian philosophy. No aspect of university life is too obscure to come under its scrutiny. The University of Connecticut issued a proclamation banning "inappropriately directed laughter" and "conspicuous exclusion of students from conversations." Did someone propose an alcohol-free "All-American Halloween Party" at Madison this fall? The majority faction in the Student Senate rose up in protest: masked students might take advantage of their anonymity to inflict "poking, pinching, rude comments" and suchlike oppressions on women and minorities. When the New York University Law School moot court board assigned a case on the custody rights of a lesbian mother, students forced its withdrawal. "Writing arguments [against the mother's side] is hurtful to a group of people and thus hurtful to all of us," one student wrote. To which Prof. Anthony Amsterdam responded: "The declaration that any legal issue is not an open question in law school is a declaration of war upon everything that a law school is." (The problem was reinstated.) At San Francisco State University, thirty students disrupted the first week of Prof. Robert Smith's course in black politics this fall. They weren't even angry about anything Smith said—they just were upset that the course had been listed in the catalog under Political Science rather than Black Studies, which they viewed as an attack on SF State's Black Studies department.

One of the most controversial PC initiatives took place at the University of Texas at Austin, where the English faculty recently chose a new text for the freshman composition course, which is required for about half of the entering undergraduates. Until now, instructors had been free to assign essays on a range of topics for students to read and discuss. Henceforth, all readings will be from an anthology called "Racism and Sexism: An Integrated Study," by Paula S. Rothenberg. The selections, some of which are excellent, comprise a primer of PC thought. In the first chapter Rothenberg answers the question that many white men wonder about but few dare ask: why are *they* the only ones ever accused of racism or sexism? The sine qua non of racism and sexism, Rothenberg explains, is *subordination,* which in Western society is exercised only by whites over blacks and men over women. Hence reverse racism and sexism by definition do not exist. Prof. Alan Gribben was one of the minority who objected to this approach to teaching composition. He derided the course as "Oppression Studies." By dictating the content of the readings, he charged, the department "presumes that content is the most important thing about the writing course." But that is just the point: in the context of PC, political content is the most important thing about everything.

What are the underpinnings of this powerful movement, so seemingly at odds with what most Americans believe?

Philosophically, PC represents the subordination of the right to free speech to the guarantee of equal protection under the law. The absolutist position on the First Amendment is that it lets you slur anyone you choose. The PC position is that a hostile environment for minorities abridges their right to an equal education. "Sure you have the right to speech," says Kate Fahey, an associate dean at Mt. Holyoke College. "But I want to know: what is it going to do to your community? Is it going to damage us?" When a few students last spring mocked Mt. Holyoke's Lesbian/Bisexual Awareness Week by proclaiming "Heterosexual Awareness Week," president Elizabeth Kennan upbraided them for violating the spirit of "community." Unfortunately for the "community," courts have generally held that highly restrictive speech codes are unconstitutional. The sociologist Ehrlich, who has written five books on racial prejudice, also considers them counterproductive. "You have to let students say the most outrageous and stupid things," he says. "To get people to think and talk, to question their own ideas, you don't regulate their speech."

Role models: But solicitude for minorities does not stop at shielding them from insults. Promotion of "diversity" is one of the central tenets of PC. Accrediting bodies have even begun to make it a condition of accreditation.

Diversity refers both to students and faculty. Of the 373 tenured professors at Harvard's Faculty of Arts and Sciences, only two are black. The latest thinking holds that black undergraduates would be less likely to drop out if there were more black teachers available to act as mentors and role models, so the competition for qualified black professors is acute.

The Ford Foundation gave grants totaling $1.6 million to 19 colleges and universities this year for "diversity." Tulane received a grant for a program "to focus the attention of . . . administration, faculty and students on the *responsibility* of each to *welcome* and *encourage* all members of the university community regardless of their race, gender, sexual orientation or religious beliefs." (Emphasis added.) That is a big responsibility. To political-science professor Paul Lewis, one of the twenty-five percent of the faculty who dissented from the university's draft "Initiatives for Race and Gender Enrichment," it implies a network of PC spies reporting to the "enrichment liaison person" in each department. Could a bad grade be construed as failure to encourage? If you don't talk to a woman you dislike, are you guilty of not making her welcome? Tulane president Eamon Kelly calls Lewis's fears "foolishness."

Politically, PC is Marxist in origin, in the broad sense of attempting to redistribute power from the privileged class (white males) to the oppressed masses. But it is Marxism of a peculiarly attenuated, self-referential kind. This is not a movement aimed at attracting more working-class youths to the university. The failure of Marxist systems throughout the world has not noticeably dimmed the allure of left-wing politics for American academics. Even today, says David Littlejohn of Berkeley's Graduate School of Literature, "an overwhelming proportion of our courses are taught by people who really hate the system."

Intellectually, PC is informed by deconstructionism, a theory of literary criticism associated with the French thinker Jacques Derrida. This accounts for the concentration of PC thought in such seemingly unlikely disciplines as comparative literature. Deconstructionism is a famously obscure theory, but one of its implications is a rejection of the notion of "hierarchy." It is impossible in deconstructionist terms to say that one text is superior to another. PC thinkers have embraced this conceit with a vengeance. "If you make any judgment or assessment as to the quality of a work, then somehow you aren't being an intellectual egalitarian," says Jean Bethke Elshtain, a political-science professor at Vanderbilt. At a conference recently she referred to Czeslaw Milosz's book "The Captive Mind" as "classic," to which another female professor exclaimed in dismay that the word *classic* "makes me feel oppressed."

Age and beauty: It is not just in literary criticism that the PC rejects "hierarchy," but in the most mundane daily exchanges as well. A Smith College handout from the Office of Student Affairs lists 10 different kinds of oppression that can be inflicted by making judgments about people. These include "ageism—oppression of the young and old by young adults and the middle-aged"; "heterosexism—oppression of those of sexual orientations other than heterosexual . . . this can take place by not acknowledging their existence," and "lookism . . . construction of a standard for beauty/attractiveness." It's not sufficient to avoid discriminating against unattractive people; you must suppress the impulse to notice the difference. But the most Orwellian category may be "ableism—oppression of the differently abled, by the temporarily able." "Differently abled" is a "term created to underline the concept that differently abled individuals are just that, not less or inferior in any way [as the terms disabled, handicapped, etc., imply]." Well, many people with handicaps surely do develop different abilities, but that is not what makes them a category. They lack something other people possess, and while that is not a reason to oppress them, it does violence to logic and language to pretend otherwise. If people could choose, how many would be "differently abled"?

Sex change: It sometimes appears that the search for euphemisms has become the great intellectual challenge of American university life. Lest anyone take offense at being called "old," he or she becomes a "non-traditional-age student." Non-Caucasians generally are "people of color." This should never be confused with "colored people." Dennis Williams, who teaches writing at Cornell, recently wrote an article on affirmative action in which he tweaked the PC with the phrase "colored students." "Students of color sounds stupid," reasoned Williams, who is black. "As language, it's sloganeering. It's like saying 'jeans of blue'." He received no comments on the substance of his article, but he got many complaints about his language—proving his point, that the form of language is taking precedence over its meaning. No one seems to have suggested renaming the sexes, although there is a movement to change the way they're spelled; at Sarah Lawrence and a few other places the PC spelling is "womyn," without the "men."

The rejection of hierarchy underlies another key PC tenet, "multiculturalism." This is an attack on the primacy of the Western intellectual tradition, as handed down through centuries of "great books." In the PC view, this canon perpetuates the power of "dead white males" over women and blacks from beyond the grave. It obliges black students to revere the thoughts of Thomas Jefferson, who was a literal slave owner. In opposition to this "Eurocentric" view of the world, Molefi Asante, chairperson of African American studies at Temple, has proposed an "Afrocentric" curriculum. It would be based on the thoughts of ancient African scholars (he annexes Pharaonic Egypt for this purpose) and the little-known (to Americans) cultures of modern East and West Africa. This would be one of many such ethnic-specific curricula he foresees in a multicultural America. "There are only two positions," Asante says sweepingly: "either you support multiculturalism in American education, or you support the maintenance of white supremacy." It is statements like that, of course, that sends members of the National Association of Scholars stomping into bookstores in a rage. To Stephen Balch, president of the organization, it is a dereliction of duty for educators to admit that every culture can be equally valid. Western civilization has earned its place at the center of the university curriculum, not by the accident that most university professors have been white males, but by its self-evident virtue. It has given rise to the single most compelling idea in human history, individual liberty, which as it happens is just now sweeping the entire world.

But Asante is proposing a change in values, not just reading lists. So what if the Western tradition gave rise to individual liberty? Is liberty necessarily a universal value? African cultures, he points out, exalt that familiar ideal: "community."

Right terms: "Community!" "Liberty!" Is there no way out of this impasse? Or are we doomed to an endless tug of war over words between the very people who should be leading us onward to a better life? If two people with as many degrees between them as Fish and Barber can't communicate except by hurling charges of "racism" and knocking over books in a store, what hope is there for the rest of us? Yet one hears the same thing over and over: I don't know how to talk to African-Americans. I'm scared of saying the wrong thing to women. Whites don't listen. "There are times when I want to be very cautious about offending a feminist colleague, but I can't find the right terms," says Robert Caserio of the University of Utah. And Caserio is an English teacher. The great Harvard sociologist David Riesman recently complained about having to go to "great lengths to avoid the tag 'racist'." "He wouldn't be annoyed to have to go to great lengths not to be anti-Semitic!" Harvard's Kilson exploded. And Riesman was once Kilson's mentor!

Yes, of course conflict is inevitable, as the university makes the transition—somewhat ahead of the rest of society—toward its multiethnic future. There are in fact some who recognize the tyranny of PC, but see it only as a transitional phase, which will no longer be necessary once the virtues of tolerance are internalized. Does that sound familiar? It's the dictatorship of the proletariat, to be followed by the withering away of the state. These should be interesting years.

Reading 2
THOUGHT REFORM 101: THE ORWELLIAN IMPLICATIONS OF TODAY'S COLLEGE ORIENTATION
Alan Charles Kors

At Wake Forest University last fall, one of the few events designated as "mandatory" for freshman orientation was attendance at *Blue Eyed*, a filmed racism awareness workshop in which whites are abused, ridiculed, made to fail, and taught helpless passivity so that they can identify with "a person of color for a day." In Swarthmore College's dormitories, in the fall of 1998, first-year students were asked to line up by skin color, from lightest to darkest, and to step forward and talk about how they felt concerning their place in that line. Indeed, at almost all of our campuses, some form of moral and political re-education has been built into freshman orientation and residential programming. These exercises have become so common-place that most students do not even think of the issues of privacy, rights, and dignity involved.

A central goal of these programs is to uproot "internalized oppression," a crucial concept in the diversity education planning documents of most universities. Like the Leninists' notion of "false consciousness," from which it ultimately is derived, it identifies as a major barrier to progressive change the fact that the victims of oppression have internalized the very values and ways of thinking by which society oppresses them. What could workers possibly know, compared to intellectuals, about what workers truly should want? What could students possibly know, compared to those creating programs for offices of student life and residence, about what students truly should feel? Any desire for assimilation or for individualism reflects the imprint of white America's strategy for racial hegemony.

In 1991 and 1992 both *The New York Times* and *The Wall Street Journal* published surveys of freshman orientations. The *Times* observed that "ori-entation has evolved into an intense . . . initiation" that involves "delicate subjects like . . . date rape [and] race relations, and how freshmen, some from small towns and tiny high schools, are supposed to deal with them." In recent years, public ridicule of "political correctness" has made academic administrators more circumspect about speaking their true minds, so one should listen carefully to the claims made for these programs before colleges began to spin their politically correct agendas.

Tony Tillman, in charge of a mandatory "Social Issues" orientation at Dartmouth, explained in the *Journal* that students needed to address "the various forms of 'isms': sexism, racism, classism," all of which were inter-related. Oberlin "educated' its freshmen about "differences in race, ethnic-ity, sexuality, gender, and culture," with separate orientations for blacks, Hispanics, gays and lesbians, and Americans of Asian descent. Columbia University sought to give its incoming students the chance "to reevaluate [and] learn things," so that they could rid themselves of "their own social and personal beliefs that foster inequality." Katherine Balmer, assistant dean for freshmen at Columbia, explained to the *Times* that "you can't bring all these people together . . . without some sort of training."

Greg Ricks, multicultural educator at Stanford (after similar stints at Dartmouth and Harvard), was frank about his agenda: "White students need help to understand what it means to be white in a multicultural community. For the white heterosexual male who feels disconnected and marginalized by multiculturalism, we've got to do a lot of work here." Planning for New Student Week at Northwestern University, a member of the Cultural Diversity Project Committee explained to the *Weekly Northwestern Review* in 1989 that the committee's goal was "changing the world, or at least the way [undergraduates] perceive it." In 1993, Ana Maria Garcia, assistant dean of Haverford College, proudly told the *Philadelphia Inquirer* of official freshman dormitory programs there, which divided students into two groups: happy, unselfish Alphas and grim, acquisitive Betas. For Garcia, the exercise was wonderfully successful: "Students in both groups said the game made them feel excluded, confused, awkward, and foolish," which, for Garcia, accomplished the purpose of Haverford's program: "to raise student awareness of racial and ethnic diversity."

In the early 1990s, Bryn Mawr College shared its mandatory "Building Pluralism" program with any school that requested it. Bryn Mawr probed the most private experiences of every first-year student: difference and discomfort; racial, ethnic, and class experiences; sexual orientation; and religious beliefs. By the end of this "orientation," students were devising "individual and collective action plans" for "breaking free" of "the cycle of oppression" and for achieving "new meaning" as "change agents." Although the public relations savvy of universities has changed since the early 1990s, these programs proliferate apace.

The darkest nightmare of the literature on power is George Orwell's *1984*, where there is not even an interior space of privacy and self. Winston Smith faces the ultimate and consistent logic of the argument that everything is political, and he can only dream of "a time when there were still privacy, love, and friendship, and when members of a family stood by one another without needing to know the reason."

Orwell did not know that as he wrote, Mao's China was subjecting university students to "thought reform," known also as "re-education," that was not complete until children had denounced the lives and political morals of their parents and emerged as "progressive" in a manner satisfactory to their trainers. In the diversity education film *Skin Deep,* a favorite in academic "sensitivity training," a white student in his third day of a "facilitated" retreat on race, with his name on the screen and his college and hometown identified, confesses his family's inertial Southern racism and, catching his breath, says to the group (and to the thousands of students who will see this film on their own campuses), "It's a tough choice, choosing what's right and choosing your family."

Political correctness is not the end of human liberty, because political correctness does not have power commensurate with its aspirations. It is essential, however, to understand those totalizing ambitions for what they are. O'Brien's re-education of Winston in *1984* went to the heart of such invasiveness. "We are not content with negative obedience . . . When finally you surrender to us, it must be of your own free will." The Party wanted not to destroy the heretic but to "capture his inner mind." Where others were content to command "Thou shalt not" or "Thou shalt," O'Brien explains, "Our command is *'Thou art'*." To reach that end requires "learning . . . understanding [and] acceptance," and the realization that one has no control even over one's inner soul. In *Blue Eyed,* the facilitator, Jane Elliott, says of those under her authority for the day, " A new reality is going to be created for these people." She informs everyone of the rules of the event: "You have no power, absolutely no power." By the end, broken and in tears, they see their own racist evil, and they love Big Sister.

The people devoted to remolding the inner lives of undergraduates are mostly kind and often charming individuals. At the Fourth Annual National Conference on People of Color in Predominantly White Institutions, held at and sponsored by the University of Nebraska last October, faculty and middle-level administrators of student life from around the country complained and joked about their low budgets, inadequate influence, and Herculean tasks. Their papers and interviews reveal an ideologically and humanly diverse crowd, but they share certain assumptions and beliefs, most of which are reasonable subjects for debate, but none of which should provide campuses with freshman agendas: America is an unjust society. Drop-out rates for students of color reflect a hostile environment and a lack of institutional understanding of identity and culture. What happens in the classroom is inadequate preparation for thinking correctly about justice and oppression.

They also share views that place us directly on the path of thought reform: White students desperately need formal "training" in racial and cultural awareness. The moral goal of such training should override white notions of privacy and individualism. The university must become a therapeutic and political agent of progressive change. Handouts at the Nebraska conclave illustrated this agenda. Inna Arnirall-Padamsee, the associate dean of student relations and the director of multicultural affairs at Syracuse University, distributed the Office of Multicultural Affairs' brochure. Its "philosophy" presupposes that students live "in a world impacted by various oppression issues," including "racism." "OMA's role," it announced, "is to provide the . . . leadership needed to encourage our students . . . to grow into individuals willing to take a proactive stance against oppression in all its shapes."

Molly Tovar, who has done this sort of work both at the University of Oklahoma and at Oklahoma State University, passed out a 22-page guide she co-authored, "How to Build and Implement a Comprehensive Diversity Plan." The guide explains the three "kinds of attitudes" that agents of cultural change will face: "The Believers," who are "cooperative; excited; participative; contributive"; "The Fence Straddlers," who are "suspicious; observers; cautious; potentially open-minded"; and "The Skeptics," who are "critical; passive aggressive; isolated; traditional."

Ronnie Wooten, of Northern Illinois University, distributed a handout, "Inclusive Classroom Matters." It adapts a variety of common academic sources on multiculturalism, including a set of "guidelines" on how to "facilitate learning about those who are different from you." The students in this "inclusive classroom" would have to abandon what might be their sincere inner beliefs, replacing them with such professions of faith as "We will assume that people (both the groups we study and the members of the class) always do the best that they can." The guidelines make it clear that one may not restrict one's changes to the intellectual: "We will address the emotional as well as the cognitive content of the course material. We will work to break down the fears that prohibit communication."

Sharon Ulmar, assistant to the chancellor for diversity and equal opportunity at the University of Nebraska at Omaha, handed out a flyer titled "Can [A] Diversity Program Create Behavior Changes?" Her program's mode of self-evaluation was to measure "the number of participants that took action based upon the awareness they learned from [the] program." Among the units of "awareness" successfully acquired were the following (some of which surely might strike one as more problematic than others): "gays and lesbians no different than [sic] others"; "handicap accessibility is for those who are handicapped [sic]"; "difficult to make a decision about own beliefs when others are watching"; "module allowed participant to witness subtle behaviors instead of hearing about it"; and the ineffably tautological "understanding commonalities of each individual may be similar to yours."

Tovar, formerly of Oklahoma State University and now at the University of Oklahoma, declares in an interview at the conference, "At OSU we have all kinds of sensitivity training." She describes an incident involving fraternity brothers who had been disrespectful of Native American culture: They ended up "incredibly emotional . . . these fraternity kids broke down." OSU also has mandatory multicultural freshman orientation sessions.

Denise Bynes, program coordinator for Adelphi University's Center for African-American Studies Programs and co-chairman of the university's Prejudice Reduction Committee, says the committee's emphasis is on training individuals how to interact "with a diverse student body," with "separate training for students . . . [and] special sessions on student leadership training." This "cultural and racial awareness training would benefit all members of the Adelphi community, both in their university and personal lives." The committee would get people to talk about " 'what I like about being so-and-so,' 'what I dislike about being so-and-so,' and 'the first time I encountered prejudice,' " all exercises that the facilitators had been shown and had experienced in their own "training" by the Justice Department.

Bynes is a kind, accomplished, candid, and well-meaning woman. As she explains, "White people must have . . . sensitivity training . . . so that they can become aware of white privilege." Mandatory sensitivity training ideally should include both students and faculty, but "there are things that we can't dictate to the faculty because of the fact that they have a union."

There are painful ironies in these attempts at thought reform. Individual identity lies at the heart of both dignity and the flourishing of an ethnically heterogeneous society. Black students on American campuses rightly decry any tendency of university police to stop students based on race. Their objections are not statistical but moral: One is an individual, not an instance of blood or appearance. The assault on individual identity was essential to the horror and inhumanity of Jim Crow laws, of apartheid, and of the Nuremberg Race Laws. It is no less inhuman when undertaken by "diversity educators." From the Inquisition to the political use of Soviet psychiatry, history has taught us to recoil morally from the violation of the ultimate refuges of self-consciousness, conscience, and private beliefs. The song of the "peat bog soldiers," sent by the Nazis to work until they died, was *"Die Gedanken sind frei"* (Thoughts Are Free), for that truly is the final atom of human liberty. No decent society or person should pursue another human being there. Our colleges and universities do so routinely. The desire to "train" individuals on issues of race and diversity has spawned a new industry of moral re-education. Colleges and universities have been hiring diversity "trainers" or "facilitators" for 15 years, and the most famous of them can command $35,000 for "cultural audits," $5,000 for sensitivity workshop training, and a sliding scale of honoraria, some for not less than $3,000 per hour, for lectures.

This growing industry has its mountebanks, its careerists, its well-meaning zealots, and its sadists. The categories often blur. Three of the most celebrated facilitators at the moment are Edwin J. Nichols, of Nichols and Associates in Washington, D.C.; Hugh Vasquez, of the Todos Institute in Oakland, California; and Jane Elliott, the Torquemada of thought reform. To examine their work is to see into the heart of American re-education.

Nichols first came to the attention of critics of intrusive political correctness in 1990, when he led an infamous "racial sensitivity" session at the University College of the University of Cincinnati. According to witnesses, his exercise culminated in the humiliation of a blond, blue-eyed, young female professor, whom he ridiculed as a "perfect" member of "the privileged white elite" who not only would win "a beauty contest" but even "wore her string of pearls." The woman, according to these accounts, sat and sobbed. These contemporaneous revelations did not harm Nichols' career.

According to the curriculum vitae sent by his firm, Nichols studied at Eberhardt-Karls Universitat in Tubingen, Germany, and at Leopold-Franzens Universitat in Innsbruck, Austria, "where he received his Doctor of Philosophy in Psychology and Psychiatry, cum laude" (a rare degree). In some publicity material, he states that he founded a school of child psychology in Africa; at other times, he modestly withholds that accomplishment.

Nichols' schedule of fees is almost as impressive as his schedule of thought reform. He charges $3,500 for a three-hour "Basic Cultural Awareness Seminar," plus travel and per diem. For a plain old "Workshop," he gets $4,000–$5,000 plus expenses. This makes his staple offering—a "Full Day Session (Awareness Seminar and Workshop)"—a bargain at $5,000 plus expenses. For a "Cultural Audit," he gets $20,000–$35,000 (he recently did one of these for the University of Michigan School of Medicine). The Bureau of Labor Statistics at the Department of Labor paid him $15,000 for diversity training; the Environmental Protection Agency got him cheaply at $12,000.

Business is booming. Nichols has brought awareness to the employees of six cabinet departments, three branches of the armed services, the Federal Reserve Bank, the Federal Aviation Administration, the Internal Revenue Service, and the FBI; the Goddard Space Center, the Naval Air Warfare Center, Los Alamos National Laboratory, and NASA; the Office of Personnel Management, the Nuclear Regulatory Commission, and the Social Security Administration. He has enlightened city and county governments, whole school systems, various state government departments, labor unions, several prestigious law firms, and the Archdiocese of Baltimore. His clients include "Fortune 500 Corporations, foreign governments, parastatals , associations, health and mental health systems," and he has been a consultant to offices of "The British Commonwealth of Nations" and "organizations in Germany, Austria, Switzerland, Japan, Latin America . . . Singapore, Malaysia, and China." He has a very long list of academic clients, and he was a centerpiece of Johns Hopkins' 1999 freshman orientation.

What does Nichols believe? He believes that culture is genetically determined, and that blacks, Hispanics, and descendants of non-Jewish Middle Eastern tribes place their "highest value" on "interpersonal relationships." In Africa, women are the equal of men. Whites were altered permanently by the Ice Age. They value objects highly, not people. That is why white men commit suicide so frequently when they are downsized.

Nichols calls his science of value systems "axiology," and he believes that if managers and administrators understand these cultural differences, they can manage more effectively, understanding why, according to him, blacks attach no importance to being on time, while whites are compulsive about it. Whites are logical; blacks are intuitive and empathetic. Whites are frigid; blacks are warm and spontaneous. Whites are relentlessly acquisitive; nonwhites are in harmony with nature. White engineers, for example, care about their part of something; Asian engineers, managers should know, care about the whole. Whites are linear; nonwhites have a spiral conception of time. Nichols has a handout that he frequently uses. Whites, it explains, "know through counting and measuring"; Native Americans learn through "oneness"; Hispanics and Arabs "know through symbolic and imagery [sic]";

Asians "know through striving toward the transcendence [sic]." Asking nonwhites to act white in the workplace is fatal to organizational harmony. Understanding cultural axiology is essential to management for the 21st century. Now, reread his list of clients.

Two diversity training films widely used at major universities reveal the techniques and the characters of two other leading thought reformers. *Skin Deep*, the 1996 film funded by the Ford Foundation, records an encounter at a retreat among college students from around the country. The facilitators are not active in the film, but the published guide tells you what they do and identifies their leader as Hugh Vasquez.

Skin Deep begins with ominous news clips from the major networks about "racial violence," "racism," "slurs," and "racist jokes" on campus. It announces that "at these training grounds for our future leaders, intolerance has once again become a way of life." We meet white, Hispanic, black, and Asian-American students from the University of Massachusetts at Amherst, the University of California at Berkeley, and Texas A&M. The whites have terrible stories to tell. They have grown up in white neighborhoods; their families have prejudices; and they feel rejected by people of color. The people of color have terrible stories to tell: They suffer frequent abuse in white America, and they are sick of it.

Neither group is typical of a college population. The whites, we gradually learn, have been members of organizations working for racial understanding. The students of color all use terms like "allies," suggesting that they've been through sessions like this before. There is a Jewish woman who objects to being thrown into the nightly "white caucus," where she doesn't really belong. She also anguishes over whether all of the things she has been told at the encounter about the Jewish role in the suffering of people of color are true. (Vasquez responds candidly to an inquiry on this, revealing that some of those allegations were outright anti-Semitic, and that the Jewish girl was looking for "allies" who would not "scapegoat" Jews.) In short, the white students talk about the stereotypes they have learned, and the students of color reflect deeply on the cruelty of race in America.

When white students initially suggest that they personally did not do terrible things, the students of color fire back with both barrels. A first reply goes immediately to the heart of the matter: "One thing that you must definitely understand is that we're discussing how this country was founded, and because you are a white male, people are going to hate you." A black student explains, more patiently: "Things are going on *presently:* the IMF, presently; the World Bank, presently; NAFTA, presently; Time Warner, presently; the diamond factories, presently; reservations, presently; ghettos, presently; barrios, presently. Slavery still exists." (Diamond factories?) The Chicana, Judy, lets them know that "I will not stop being angry, and I will not be less angry or frustrated to accommodate anybody. You whites have to understand because we have been oppressed for 2,000 years. And if you take offense, so?" (Two thousand years?) And from Khanh, a bitter Vietnamese student: "White people need to hear that white people are very affected by internalized racism. As a person of color growing up in this society, I was taught to hate myself and I did hate myself. If you're a white person, you were taught to love yourself. If you don't know that, you have shit in your head; you'll never deal with racism."

By the end, the students of color have had the grace to state that if the white students become real "allies," their victims can let go of their anger a bit. White students have come to realize that the pieties their parents taught them, such as an honest day's pay for an honest day's work, apply only to whites in America.

In short, what moves the film (and American thought reform) is a denial of individual identity and responsibility, an insistence on group victimization and rights, and the belief that America is an almost uniquely iniquitous place in the world, without opportunity, legal equality, or justice. "I want you to know," a Hispanic male explains, "that because of the system, my cousin was shot . . . and then another cousin was shot." The tribalism of the exploited Third World expresses a core truth: You are your blood and history. Let the children of the guilty denounce their parents. Let the victims stake their claims. Let the cultural revolution begin. Vasquez is a frank and warm man by e-mail. He explains that the filmmaker never showed the facilitators because she wanted to focus solely on the students, but that "it took a great deal of planning and structure and facilitation to make what happened happen." In his own mind, he was devoted to eliminating "blame, ridicule, judgments, guilt, and shame" among all of the students in the group, and he sounds sincere when he writes that his goal is to eliminate "individual and institutional mistreatment of any group or culture." But his effect, whatever his intention, is frightening, atavistic, and irrational, and his means are deeply intrusive. Americans surely need to study, discuss, and debate, frankly, matters of race and ethnicity. Reasonable people disagree on profound questions. Some of the issues are empirical: Is aversion to difference acquired above all from culture or evolution? Should we be more startled by America's success in creating a nation of diverse backgrounds or by the difficulties it has in doing so?

Some of the issues are moral and political: Should we favor legal equality with differential outcomes or equality of outcomes even at the price of legal inequality? Are today's whites responsible for the crimes of 19th-century Southern slave owners? What are the benefits and costs of a society based on individual responsibility? These are not issues for indoctrination. Indeed, they do not even reflect everyone's chosen intellectual or moral agenda, and free individuals choose such agendas for themselves.

Vasquez's "Study Guide" for *Skin Deep* explains that the final goal of using the film in "colleges, high schools, corporations, and the workplace" is to produce "action strategies and . . . networks for working against

racism," for which there is a page of strategy. The guide further explains the
necessity of affirmative action, the "myths" of reverse discrimination and
balkanization, and the reality of white privilege. It teaches the need for the
privileged to become "allies" of the oppressed, and it focuses on the nightmare of "internalized oppression." The internalization of oppression manifests itself in "self-doubt . . . fear of one's own power; an urgent pull to
assimilate; isolation from one's own group; self-blame for lack of success;
[and] fighting over the smallest slice of the economic pie."

The guide also has a rare explicit endorsement of "political correctness,"
reminding facilitators that "language was a prime factor" in the murder of
6 million Jews, that language perpetuates racism, and that it is wrong to
believe that "anything people say should be left alone simply because we all
have the right to free speech . . . The challenges to political correctness
tend to come from those who want to be able to say anything without
repercussions." (He did not have Khanh in mind.)

Skin Deep is a kid's cartoon, however, compared to Jane Elliott's *Blue
Eyed*. Elliott has been lionized by the American media, including Oprah
Winfrey, and she is widely employed by a growing number of universities.
Disney plans to make a movie of her life. *Blue Eyed* arose from Elliott's
elementary school class in Riceville, Iowa, where, starting in 1968, she
inflicted upon her dyslexic students an experience in which they were
loathed or praised based upon their eye color. According to Elliott, she was
ostracized for this experiment, her own children were beaten and abused,
and her parents (who were racists, she informed a Dutch interviewer) were
driven into isolation, bankruptcy, and despair because they had raised
"a nigger lover" (one of her favorite terms).

In her modest explanation, once news of her exercise with the children
made it onto national television, the people of Riceville feared that blacks
across America would assume that everyone there was like Elliott and
would move to their town. To punish her for that, they stopped buying
from her father. Elliott also revealed to her Dutch interviewer that she
abandoned teaching school in 1984 to devote herself full time to diversity
education, for which she receives $6,000 per day from "companies and
governmental institutions."

In *Blue Eyed*, masochistic adults accept Elliott's two-and-a-half-hour
exercise in sadism (reduced to 90 minutes of film), designed to make white
people understand what it is to be "a person of color" in America.
To achieve this, she divides her group into stupid, lazy, shiftless, incompetent,
and psychologically brutalized "blue eyes," on the one hand, and clever
and empowered "brown eyes," on the other. Some of the sadism is central
to the "game," but much is gratuitous, and it continues after the exercise
has ended.

Elliott is unbearably tendentious and ignorant. To teach what an IQ test
truly is, she gives the brown eyes half of the answers to an impossible test

before the blue eyes enter the room, explaining that, for people of color, the IQ exam is "a test about which you know absolutely nothing." IQ tests only measure "white culture." They are a means of "reinforcing our position of power," and "we do this all the time in public, private, and parochial schools," using "culturally biased tests, textbooks, and pictures on the wall . . . for white people." (Fortunately for Elliott, it appears there were no Asian-Americans or psychometricians in her group.)

Elliott often describes the 1990s as if they were the 1920s; indeed, in her view, nothing has changed in America since the collapse of Reconstruction. Every day in the United States, she explains, white power keeps black males in their place by calling them "boy" (two syllables, hissed), "and we do it to accomplished black males over 70, and we get away with it." We tell blacks to assimilate, which means merely to "act white," but when they try that, we put them in their place and change the rules. For example (this in 1995), whites now are building up Colin Powell, but as soon as they build "this boy" up, they will kick him down. For Elliott, the Powell boom was a conscious conspiracy to humiliate and disorient blacks.

She teaches her "blueys" with relish that protest accomplishes nothing, because if blacks protest, "we kill them." It is not smart to speak up or act clever, which is why blacks appear passive and stupid. The lesson: "You have no power, absolutely no power. . . . Quit trying." Blacks might try to "win" on the inside, but it is almost impossible to validate oneself when white society puts you down "all day, every day."

Even if a "bluey" understands the implications of the workshop, or even if a white woman understands male prejudice, it bears no real relationship to the daily suffering of every black: "You do not live in the same country as that [black] woman. You live in the USA, but you do not live in the same country as she does." Blacks such as Shelby Steele (singled out by name), who speak of transcending race, delude themselves, because one might transcend one's skin color but never society's behavior: "All you can do is sit there and take it." People call the exercise cruel, Elliott explains, but "I'm only doing this for one day to little white children. Society does this to children of color every day." She stands over briefly assertive "blueys" and humiliates them, explaining that if this makes you sick to your stomach for a few hours, now you understand why blacks die younger.

In short, this is America, and there truly is no hope. Nothing ever changes. No one can succeed by effort. Culture, society, and politics all are static. "White privilege" controls all agencies of power, influence, and image, and uses all the means that arise from these to render "people of color" psychologically impotent, confused, passive, and helpless. So either vent your hatred or assume your guilt.

There is no redemption except guilt, but there is a political moral. After "teaching" a "bluey" to submit totally to her authority, she asks if that was a good lesson. The workshop thinks it was. No, she says with venom, submission to tyranny is a terrible lesson, but "what I just did to him today Newt Gingrich is doing to you every day . . . and you are submitting to that, submitting to oppression."

The facilitators' guide and publicity for *Blue Eyed* states things honestly: Elliott "does not intellectualize highly emotionally charged or challenging topics . . . she uses participants' own emotions to make them feel discomfort, guilt, shame, embarrassment, and humiliation." Facilitators are urged to use the raw emotions of *Blue Eyed* (blueys do cry a lot) to tap the reactions of the viewers. They should not expect black participants to "bleed on the floor for whites," but they should get whites to "stretch" and "take risks." The facilitators should be prepared for very strong and painful emotions and memories from the participants. The ultimate goal of the film: "It is not enough for white people to stop abusing people of color. All U.S. people need a personal vision for ending racism and other oppressive ideologies within themselves."

Elliott does mean everyone. In 1996, she told her audience at Kansas State University that all whites are racists, whatever they believe about themselves: "If you want to see another racist, turn to the person on your right. Now look at the person on your left." She also believes that blacks were in America 600 years before whites. She told the students at Kansas State that if they were angry at her, they should write letters, but that they must do so without paper, alphabet, or numbers, all of which were invented by people of color. Whites, in Elliott's view, did have certain creativity. Betraying a breathtaking ignorance of world history, she told the Australian Internet magazine *Webfronds* in 1998 that "white people invented racism." Other than that, however, whites were quite parasitic.

"You're all sitting here writing in a language [English] that white people didn't come up with," she told the magazine. "You're all sitting here writing on paper that white people didn't invent. Most of you are wearing clothes made out of cloth that white people didn't come up with. We stole those ideas from other people. If you're a Christian, you're believing in a philosophy that came to us from people of color."

Jane Elliott has lived through revolutionary cultural changes without taking note of any. She teaches only helplessness and despair to blacks and only blood-guilt and self-contempt to whites. She addresses no issue with intellectual seriousness or purpose. She also is the reigning star in thought reform these days. On May 7, 1999, CBS News ran a feature on her that declared: "For over 30 years, Jane Elliott has waged a one-woman campaign against racism in America." CBS might want to rethink the notion of "racism."

Even traditionalist campuses now permit the ideologues in their offices of student life to pursue individuals into the last inner refuge of free men and women and to turn students over to trainers who want them to change "within themselves." This is a return of *in loco parentis,* with a power unimagined in prior ages by the poor souls who only tried to keep men and women from sleeping with each other overnight. It is the university standing not simply in the place of parents but in the place of private conscience, identity, and belief.

From the evidence, most students tune it out, just as most students at most times generally have tuned out abuses of power and diminutions of liberty. One should not take heart from that. Where students react, it is generally with an anger that, ironically and sadly, exacerbates the balkanization of our universities. The more social work we bring to our colleges and universities, the more segregated they become, and in the classifieds of *The Chronicle of Higher Education* during the last few years, colleges and universities by the hundreds have advertised for individuals to oversee "diversity education," "diversity training," and "sensitivity training."

Orwell may have been profoundly wrong about the totalitarian effects of high technology, but he understood full well how the authoritarians of this century had moved from the desire for outer control to the desire for inner control. He understood that the new age sought to overcome what, in Julia's terms, was the ultimate source of freedom for human beings: "They can't get inside you." Our colleges and universities hire trainers to "get inside" American students.

Thought reform is making its way inexorably to an office near you. If we let it occur at our universities and accept it passively in our own domains, then a people who defeated totalitarians abroad will surrender their dignity, privacy, and conscience to the totalitarians within.

Alan Charles Kors (akors@sas.upenn.edu) is a professor of history at the University of Pennsylvania, co-author of *The Shadow University: The Betrayal of Liberty on America's Campuses* (HarperCollins), and president of FIRE, the Foundation for Individual Rights in Education. He is indebted to Thor Halvorssen, executive director of FIRE, for the materials and interviews from the Nebraska conference.

Reading 3
WHY WESTERN HISTORY MATTERS
Donald Kagan

In 1990, I suggested to the freshmen of Yale College that they would be wise to make the study of Western civilization the center of their pursuit of a liberal education. I pointed out the devastating effects of ethnic conflict and disunity around the world and the special problems and opportunities confronting the U.S., a country that was never a nation in the sense of resting on common ancestry but one that depends on a set of beliefs and institutions deriving from Western traditions. I argued that the unity of our country and the defense of its freedom required that its citizens understand the ideas, history, and traditions that created them.

The debate that followed revealed a broad and deep ignorance of the historical process by which the very values that encourage current criticisms of the Western experience came into being.

Western civilization was not the result of some inevitable process through which other cultures will automatically pass. It emerged from a unique history in which chance and accident played a vital part. The institutions and ideas that provide for freedom and improvement in material conditions cannot flourish without an understanding of how they came about.

The many civilizations adopted by the human race have shared basic characteristics. Most have tended toward cultural uniformity and stability. Reason, though employed for all sorts of practical and intellectual purposes, lacked independence from religion and the high status to challenge the most basic received ideas. The standard form of government has been monarchy. Religious and political institutions and beliefs have been thoroughly intertwined in a mutually supportive unified structure; government has not been subject to secular, reasoned analysis.

The first and sharpest break with this common experience came in ancient Greece. The Greek city-states were republics. There were no kings with the wealth to hire mercenary soldiers, so the citizens did their own fighting. As independent defenders of the common safety and interest, they demanded a role in the most important political decisions; in this way, for the first time, political life came to be shared by a relatively large portion of the people.

What most set the Greeks apart was their view of the world. The Greek way of looking at things requires a change from the use of faith, poetry, and intuition to a reliance on reason. The Greeks exposed everything they perceived—natural, human, and divine—to the searching examination of logos.

But the Greeks combined a unique sense of mankind's possibilities with a painful understanding of its limitations. This is the tragic vision of the human condition that characterized classical Greek civilization. To cope with it, they urged human beings to restrain their over-arching ambitions. Inscribed at Apollo's temple at Delphi were the slogans "know thyself" and "nothing in excess."

Beyond these exhortations they relied on a good political regime to train human beings in virtue and restrain them from vice. Aristotle made the point neatly:

"As man is the best of the animals when perfected, so he is the worst when separated from law and justice. For injustice is most dangerous when it is armed, and man, armed by nature with good sense and virtue, may use them for entirely opposite ends. Therefore, when he is without virtue man is the most unscrupulous and savage of the animals."

The second great strand in the history of the West is the Judeo-Christian tradition. Christianity's main roots were in Judaism, a religion that worships a single, all-powerful deity who is sharply separated from human beings, makes great moral demands upon them, and judges them all, even kings and emperors. Christianity began as a persecuted religion that captured the Roman Empire only after centuries of hostility, and it never entirely lost its original character as an insurgent movement, independent of the state and hostile to it.

The union of a universalist religion with a monarch such as the Roman emperor, who ruled a vast empire, could nevertheless have put an end to any prospect of freedom. But Christianity's inheritance of the rational, disputatious Greek philosophy led to powerfully divisive quarrels about the nature of God and other theological questions.

The Barbarians' destruction of the Western Empire also destroyed the power of the emperors and their efforts to impose religious and political conformity under imperial control. Here we arrive at a second sharp break with the general experience of mankind. The West of the Germanic tribes that had toppled the Roman Empire was weak and divided. Nobody sought or planned for freedom, but in the space left by the endless conflicts among secular rulers and between them and the church, there was room for freedom to grow.

Into some of that space towns and cities reappeared. Taking advantage of the rivalries mentioned above, they obtained charters from the local powers establishing their right to govern themselves. In Italy some of these cities were able to gain control of the surrounding country and to become city-states resembling those of ancient Greece.

In these states the modern world began to take form. Although the people were Christian, their life and outlook became increasingly secular. Here, and in other cities north of the Alps, arose a worldview that celebrated the greatness and dignity of mankind. Its vision is revealed with flamboyant confidence by Pico della Mirandola. He wrote that God told man:

"We have made thee neither of heaven nor of earth, neither mortal nor immortal, so that with freedom of choice and with honor, as though the maker and molder of thyself, thou mayest fashion thyself in whatever shape thou shalt prefer . . . O supreme generosity of God the Father, O highest and most felicity of man! To him is granted to have whatever he chooses, to be whatever he wills."

This is a remarkable leap beyond the humanism of the Greeks, something new in the world. Man is more than mortal, unlimited by nature, entirely free to shape himself and to acquire whatever he wants.

Another Florentine, Machiavelli, moved further in the same directions. For him "Fortune is a woman, . . . and it is necessary to hold her down and beat her and fight with her," a notion the Greeks would have regarded as dangerously arrogant and certain to produce disaster.

Francis Bacon, influenced by Machiavelli, urged human beings to employ their reason to force nature to give up its secrets. He assumed that such a course would lead to progress and the general improvement of the human condition. Such thinking lay at the heart of the scientific revolution and remains the faith on which modern science and technology rest.

Hobbes and Locke applied a similar novelty and modernity to the sphere of politics, discovering "natural rights" that belong to man either as part of nature or as the gifts of a benevolent and reasonable God. Man's basic rights—life, liberty, and property—were seen as absolute.

Freedom was threatened in early modern times by the emergence of monarchies, but the cause of individual liberty was enhanced by the Protestant Reformation, another upheaval within Christianity arising from its focus on individual salvation, its inheritance of a tradition of penetrating reason, and the continuing struggle between church and state.

The English Revolution came about in large part because of Charles I's attempt to impose an alien religious conformity, as well as tighter political control, on his kingdom. In England the tradition of freedom and government bound by law was strong enough to produce effective resistance. From the ensuing rebellion came limited, constitutional, representative government and, ultimately, democracy. The example and the ideas it produced encouraged and informed the French and American revolutions and the entire modern constitutional tradition.

These ideas and institutions are the basis for modern liberal thinking about politics, the individual, and society, just as the confident view of science and technology as progressive forces has been the most powerful form taken by the Western elevation of reason. In the last two centuries both these elements of Western civilization have come under heavy attack. At different times, science and technology have been blamed for the destruction of human community and the alienation of people from nature and from one another, for intensifying the gulf between rich and poor, for threatening the very existence of humanity either by producing weapons of total destruction or by destroying the environment.

At the same time, the foundations of freedom have also come into question. Jefferson and his colleagues could confidently proclaim their political rights as the gift of a "Creator." By now, however, the power of religion has faded, and for many the basis for a modern political and moral order has been demolished. Nietzsche announced the death of God, and Dostoevsky's Grand Inquisitor asserted that when God is dead all things are permitted. Nihilism rejects any objective basis for society and its morality, the very concept of objectivity, even the possibility of communication itself, and a vulgar form of nihilism has a remarkable influence in our educational system today.

The consequences of the victory of such ideas would be enormous. If both religion and reason are removed, all that remains is will and power, where the only law is that of tooth and claw. There is no protection for the freedom of weaker individuals or those who question the authority of the most powerful. There is no basis for individual rights or for a critique of existing ideas and institutions.

That such attacks on the greatest achievements of the West should be made by Western intellectuals is perfectly in keeping with the Western tradition, yet it seems ironic that they have gained so much currency at the height of the achievements of Western reason in the form of science, and at a moment when its concept of political freedom seems to be sweeping all before it.

Still, we cannot deny that there is a dark side to the Western experience. To put untrammeled reason and individual freedom at the center of a civilization is to live with the turmoil that they produce. Freedom was born and has survived in the space created by divisions and conflict within and between nations and religion. We must wonder whether the power of modern weapons will allow it and the world to survive at such a price. Individual freedom, although it greatly elevates the condition of the people who live in free societies, inevitably permits inequalities that are the more galling because each person is plainly responsible for the outcome. Freedom does permit isolation from society and an alienation of the individual at a high cost to both.

Nor are these the only problems posed by the Western tradition in its modern form. Whether it takes the form of the unbridled claims of Pico della Mirandola, or of the Nietzschean assertion of the power of the superior individual to shape his own nature, or of the modern totalitarian effort to change humanity by utopian social engineering, the temptation to arrogance threatens the West's traditions and achievements.

Because of Western civilization's emergence as the exemplary civilization, it also presents problems to the whole world. The challenges presented by freedom and reason cannot be met by recourse to the experience of other cultures, where these characteristics have not been prominent. To understand and cope without problems we all need to know and to grapple with the Western experience.

In my view, we need especially to examine the older traditions of the West—especially among the Greeks, who began it all. They understood the potentiality of human beings, their limitations, and the predicament in which they live. Man is potent and important, yet he is fallible and mortal, capable of the greatest achievements and the worst crimes. He is a tragic figure, powerful but limited, with freedom to choose and all but bound by his own nature, knowing that he will never achieve perfect knowledge and understanding, justice and happiness, but determined to continue the search.

To me that seems an accurate description of the human condition that is meaningful not only for the Greeks and their heirs in the West but for all human beings. It is an understanding that cannot be achieved without a serious examination of the Western experience. The abandonment of such a study or its adulteration for current political purposes would be a terrible loss to all of humanity.

Donald Kagan is Bass Professor of History and Classics and Western Civilization at Yale University, New Haven, CT 06520.

Reading 4
WHERE THE BOYS ARE
Christina Hoff Sommers

This reading is a Bradley Lecture delivered at the American Enterprise Institute, November 9, 1998.

I am Christina Hoff Sommers, W.H. Brady Fellow at the American Enterprise Institute. For most of my professional career I have been writing on ethics and moral philosophy. I have also written extensively about the influence of feminism on American culture. I will talk to you about some themes in a book called *The War against Boys*. I will tell you something about how boys and girls are faring educationally and otherwise. There is a lot of misinformation on this topic. Too many advocacy groups are shaping the discussion and painting their own alarming pictures. I will try to give you the best and most up-to-date information on the true state of affairs. Of course, information is never the whole story. I too have a point of view, and I will tell you about that as well.

There is a story making the rounds in education circles, about a now-retired Chicago public school teacher, Mrs. Dougherty. Mrs. Dougherty was a dedicated, highly respected sixth grade teacher, who could always be counted on to bring the best out in her students. But one year she had a class she found impossible to control. The students were rowdy, unmanageable, and seemingly un-teachable. She began to worry that many of them had serious learning disabilities—or mental disorders—or something. So one day when the principal was out of town, she did something teachers were forbidden to do in that school. She entered the principal's office and looked into the special files that listed students' IQs. To her shock she found a majority of the class was way above average in intelligence. A large cluster was in the high 120s: 128, 127, 129; several scored in the 130s; and one of the worst classroom culprits was in fact brilliant. He had an IQ of 145.

Well, Mrs. Dougherty was furious. She had been feeling sorry for those kids, giving them remedial work and making excuses for them. Things were about to change. She went back to her class and a new era began. She read them the riot act. They would comport themselves like ladies and gentlemen. She doubled the homework load, raised the standards, gave draconian punishments to any malefactor. Slowly but perceptibly their performance began to improve. By the end of the year, this class of ne'er-do-wells was the best behaved and highest performing of all the sixth grade classes.

The principal was of course delighted. He knew about this class and its reputation for incorrigibility. And one day he called her into his office and asked her: What did you do? She felt compelled to tell him the truth. She confessed that when he had been out of town, she had looked up children's IQs.

The principal forgave her. Congratulated her. Then he said something surprising: "I think you should know, Mrs. Dougherty—those numbers, next to the children's names, they're not IQ scores, they're their locker numbers."

I heard this story from Dr. Carl Boyd, who is president of an educational foundation in Kansas City. He says the story is true, and I believe him. The moral for teachers is obvious: demand and expect excellence from students and you'll get the best they can give. Be tough on them. Be like Mrs. Dougherty.

Some of you may think that this is self-evident, that it's only common sense. Who questions setting and enforcing high standards for students? The answer is a lot of education experts. Many professors and deans at our leading schools have convinced themselves and others that American children are vulnerable, fragile, and in crisis. They believe children are harmed by teachers who enforce high standards. They want teachers to pay attention to the child's self-esteem and emotional stability. The fashion in many classrooms is for teachers to break the class up into small, non-threatening, cooperative learning groups—the teacher is more of a supportive facilitator rather than a demanding taskmaster. In the early nineties it was the girls who were portrayed as being at special risk, in need of a therapeutic pedagogy; now it's the boys as well.

My own view is that the child-crisis is a myth. And I believe that taking a therapeutic approach to education is a very bad idea for all students. But, as I shall try to show, it is especially harmful to boys. The idea that our children are fragile, being harmed by the dominant culture that forces them into feminine or masculine gender stereotypes, is now the fashion in education. Let me tell you who promoted and popularized this idea and then give you my reasons for rejecting it.

The girl-crisis came first and a single professor at Harvard University is the person most responsible for promulgating it. In 1989, Carol Gilligan, a professor at the Harvard School of Education and a pioneer in the field of women's psychology, announced her finding that the nation's adolescent girls were in crisis. In her words, "As the river of a girl's life flows into the sea of Western culture, she is in danger of drowning or disappearing." Gilligan believes girls are silenced—"they lose their voice" as they enter adolescence in our male-centered society. Her distressing portrait of endangered girls had no basis in reality, as I shall show. But it fascinated an uncritical media who helped gain for it a widespread acceptance.

Soon after Gilligan issued her admonition about our drowning, silenced, and disappearing daughters, feminist researchers and women's advocacy groups began reporting that the nation's teenaged girls are academically "shortchanged," drained of their self-esteem by a society that favors boys. The American Association of University Women called what was happening to girls "an unacknowledged American tragedy." The state of the nation's girls was being described in increasingly lurid terms. A *Los Angeles Times* writer talked of the "widespread process of psychic suicide among ordinary teenage girls." Here is Mary Pipher in *Reviving Ophelia: Saving the Selves of Adolescent Girls* (this book stayed high on the *New York Times* best-seller list for more than one year). According to Pipher:

Something dramatic happens to girls in early adolescence. Just as planes and ships disappear mysteriously into the Bermuda Triangle, so do the selves of girls go down in droves. They crash and burn.

The allegedly low state of America's girls moved the United States Congress to pass the Gender Equity Act, categorizing girls as an "under-served population" on a par with other discriminated-against minorities. Millions in grants were awarded to study the plight of girls and to learn how to cope with the insidious bias against them. At the Fourth World Conference on Women in Beijing, the American delegation presented the educational and psychological deficits of American girls as a pressing human rights issue.

Later in the '90s, the crisis talk would turn to boys. Here again Gilligan is a moving spirit. She claims to have found that boys too are traumatized by the way they are "socialized" in what she calls the "patriarchal social order." She and some of her male disciples in the New England area are promoting a movement to rescue boys from the hostile male culture that is harming them. You may already have noticed a lot of recent stories about the crashing "selves" of boys. On June 4, 1998, McLean Hospital, the psy-chiatric teaching hospital of the Harvard Medical School, issued a two-page press release announcing the results of a new study on boys. The study, enti-tled "Listening to Boys' Voices," was conducted by Dr. William Pollack, Director of the Center for Men at McLean Hospital and assistant professor of psychology at Harvard. Pollack's conclusions are sweeping and alarming. He says that even seemingly normal boys are "in trouble"—they are "dis-connected," unable to relate to people and unable to express emotions. Echoing the talk of girls as Ophelias, Pollack refers to American boys as "young Hamlets [who] succumb to an inner state of Denmark. "He urges immediate action on a nationwide scale: "[A]s a nation, we must address these boys' pain before it reaches epidemic proportions and severely disrupts our society."

Stories about the boy crisis appeared in a number of leading newspapers— *The New York Times, The Washington Post,* the *Boston Globe*—the crisis made the cover of *Newsweek* and was the subject of an ABC 20/20 segment; the *Today* show devoted two programs to it.

Gilligan, Pipher, Pollack, and their many colleagues speak of saving, rescuing, reviving. By using Ophelia and Hamlet as symbols, the child crisis writers offer a dark and unwholesome portrait of America's girls and boys. But is it accurate? Is it helpful? Are American children well served by being portrayed as tragic and psychologically ailing? My answer to all three questions is an emphatic no.

The first thing to notice is that none of the crisis writers has published their alarming findings in any peer-reviewed social science journals. Bypassing the scrutiny of peer review, both Gilligan and Pollack simply announced their conclusions in the popular press.

More conventional scholars, who abide by the protocols of respectable social science research, see no evidence of crisis. Dr. Anne Peterson, a University of Minnesota "adolescent psychologist," reports the consensus of clinicians and researchers working in adolescent psychology:

It is now known that the majority of adolescents of both genders successfully negotiate this developmental period without any major psychological or emotional disorder, develop a positive sense of personal identity, . . . and manage to forge adaptive peer relationships at the same time they maintain close relationships with their families.

Daniel Offer, the University of Michigan Professor of Psychiatry, refers to "a new generation of studies" that find a majority of adolescents [80%] normal and well-adjusted." Just consider the contrast between William Pollack's study with its finding that seemingly healthy boys are really distraught and desperate and Daniel Offer's article with its finding that most adolescents—male or female—are psychically sound.

Offer's article is published in a professional journal—the *Journal of American Child Adolescence*. His data are available. He supports his thesis by referencing more than 150 other peer-reviewed journal articles. He clearly states his methodology. He carefully explains the scope and limitations of his study.

William Pollack's study (which I obtained by requesting it from McLean Hospital's public relations office) is a 30-page typed manuscript. It has never been published and is not marked as about to be published. The manuscript contains not a single footnote—not a single reference to other work. His conclusions about boys are based mainly on some psychological and gender awareness tests he administered to 150 middle school boys. We are not told how he selected these boys, or whether they constitute anything like a representative sample. As far as stating its own limitations, Dr. Pollack declares, "These findings are unprecedented in the literature of research psychology." When Francis Crick and James Watson announced their epochal discovery of the double helix in the British journal *Nature,* they were calmer than Dr. Pollack.

As for Professor Gilligan, she has not published her data on "drowning and disappearing" girls in social science journals. The pronouncement that girls were endangered was made in a book called *Making Connections: The Relational Worlds of Adolescent Girls at Emma Willard School.*

Gilligan's central thesis is that as girls enter adolescence, they lose their "voice"—their expressiveness and confidence. What empirical basis does she have for this claim? Gilligan and her colleagues interviewed a hundred or so boarding school girls about how they felt growing into adolescence. Gilligan explains in the prologue of *Making Connections* that the studies in the collection are not intended as a "definitive statement about girls." Instead, "they are offered in the spirit of celebration . . ." (p. 5).

Contrast Gilligan's work with the less celebratory, but more conventional research of Susan Harter of the University of Denver. Harter and her associates attempted to test Gilligan's hypothesis that girls lose their expressiveness, their "voice," as they enter adolescence. Unlike Gilligan, Harter published her findings in a peer reviewed professional journal, *Educational Psychologist*. Gilligan interviewed 100 girls at the Emma Willard School. Harter interviewed (approximately) 900 male and female students from grades 6–12 and from a range of economic backgrounds and school types. We learn little about the sort of questions Gilligan asked the girls. Harter, on the other hand, clearly explains her interview instrument and how it was tested for internal consistency. She notes its limitations.

What did Harter find? "There is no evidence in our data for a loss of voice among female adolescents." She could not even find a trend in that direction. She and her co-investigators have now done several studies that appear to disconfirm Gilligan's findings. They are careful to say that these are inconclusive and that Gilligan's predictions about loss of voice might be true for a subset of girls in certain domains. They suggest that more work needs to be done. But for the time being, Harter cautions "against generalizations about either gender as a group."

Journalists speak of Gilligan's "landmark research" but they never ask whether this research exists; nor do they ask her any critical questions. *Education Week* recently asked me what I thought of Gilligan's work and claims. I said, "I think she is an engaging and imaginative writer, but I'm not sure what she does has much status as social science." *Education Week* reported Gilligan's response to my remarks:

[I]f quantitative studies are the only kind that qualify as research, then Charles Darwin, the father of evolutionary theory, would not be considered a researcher.

Even the most cursory look at Gilligan's so-called landmark research in developmental psychology suggests that comparisons to Darwin may be premature.

What I believe is that the child-crisis writers are irresponsibly portraying healthy American girls and boys as pathological victims of an inimical culture. Why does the public indulge them? It should be said that pathologizing large groups of average people is something we Americans are all too fond of doing. In an article entitled "A Nation of Nuts" *New York Observer* editor Jim Windolf tallied the number of Americans who are said to be suffering from a mental disorder. According to estimates of various experts and advocacy groups, 15 million Americans suffer from social anxiety. Ten million have seasonal affective disorder. Five hundred thousand are victims of chronic fatigue syndrome. Multiple chemical sensitivity afflicts 2.5 million; borderline personality disorder, 10 million; manic depression, 2 million. Another 5.4 million have obsessive compulsive disorder. Windolf concludes:

If you believe the statistic, 77% of America's adult population is a mess. And we haven't even thrown in abductees, road-ragers or Internet addicts.

The child crisis writers fit right in. Except they are more extreme. If you credit the startling and alarming claims of Pipher, Gilligan, Pollack, and the other child-doomsayers, American adults turn out to be paragons of psychic well-being compared to all the anguished child Hamlets and shattered child Ophelias in our midst.

So far I have been inveighing against the large, extreme, and irresponsible claims of the crisis writers, and I suggested that they have produced no credible evidence to back them up. Now let me consider some of their more moderate and seemingly reasonable assertions. Let's consider the suggestion that boys are emotionally repressed, out of touch with their own feelings. Is that true? And should we be concerned? Gilligan speaks of boys as "hid[ing] their humanity" and submerging "their very best qualities . . . their sensitivity." Are boys insensitive?

One thing is undeniable: Stereotypical boy behavior that was once considered normal now offends and upsets a lot of people. In the fall of 1997, I took part in a television debate with feminist lawyer Gloria Allred in which we disagreed over male and female differences. I pointed out that younger boys and girls have markedly different preferences and behaviors, citing the following homespun example. Hasbro Toys, a major toy company, tested a playhouse they were considering marketing to both boys and girls. They soon discovered that girls and boys did not interact with the structure in the same way. The girls dressed the dolls, talked to them, kissed them, and played house; the boys catapulted the baby carriage from the roof. I said to Ms. Allred, "Surely you would agree, boys and girls are innately different?"

Allred seemed to be shocked by the boys' catapulting behavior. Apparently, she takes it as a sign of a propensity for violence. She flatly denied there were any innate differences. Said Allred, "If there are little boys who catapult baby carriages off the roof of doll houses that is just one more reason why we have to socialize boys at an earlier age, perhaps to be playing with dollhouses."

A second example of worrying and (apparently) offensive boy behavior: Ms. Logan is a very committed middle school teacher in San Francisco who sees it as her mission to sensitize boys, to make them more aware of how women have been oppressed, and at the same time to bring out their more loving, nurturing side. As a class assignment she has the children make a quilt celebrating "women we admire." But there is a problem; the boys do not always produce the kind of muslin quilt squares the teacher wants. There are worrying signs of persistent insensitivity. A 12-year-old boy named Jimmy, for example, chose to honor the tennis player Monica Seles by drawing a bloody knife on a tennis racket. It's not the sort of thing a girl would think of. Jimmy's square may be unique in the history of quilting but Ms. Logan did not appreciate its originality. She insisted he start again and make an acceptable contribution to the class quilt.

I am afraid my own 14-year-old son, David, provides yet another example of male insensitivity and inadequate emotional engagement. *Write Source 2000* is a widely used middle school English textbook by Houghton-Mifflin: 1.5 million copies have been sold, which means a lot of children use them. Like many other contemporary reading and grammar textbooks, *Write Source 2000* is chock full of exercises designed to improve children's self-esteem and to draw them out emotionally. My son came to me one evening confused by his homework assignment. He asked, "Mom, what do they want?" He had read a short story in which one character always compared himself to another. Here were the questions David had to answer:

Do you often compare yourself with others? Do you compare to make yourself feel better? Does your comparison ever make you feel inferior?

Another set of questions asked about profanity in the story:

• How did cursing make you feel? Do you curse? Why?
• Does cursing make you feel more powerful? Are you feeling a bit uneasy about discussing cursing? Why? Why not?

The *Write Source 2000 Teacher's Guide* (which I sent away for) suggests grading students on a scale from l-to-l0: a "ten" for students who are "intensely engaged"; a "one" "does not engage at all." My son did not engage. Here is how he answered:

Do you often compare yourself to someone else?
"Sometimes."
Do you compare to make yourself feel better?
"No. I do not."
Do your comparisons make you feel inferior?
"No."

Boys catapulting baby carriages off roofs. Jimmy and the bloody knife on his quilt patch, my son and his laconic disengaged homework answers—are such behaviors symptomatic of emotional repression—are they warning signs of potential violence? Carol Gilligan thinks so. She recently told *The New York Times* that boys are cut off emotionally; she speaks of boys as repressing "humanity" and learning to "hurt without feeling hurt." Pollack thinks so. He says boys are disconnected, isolated, alienated, and trapped by a stereotypical masculinity that prevents them from expressing their painful inner feelings. He speaks of the recent school shootings as the tip of the iceberg.

It is undeniable that a small subset of boys fit the Gilligan/Pollack description of being desensitized and cut off from feelings of tenderness and care. But the vast majority of boys are no more antisocial than their female counterparts. Nevertheless, the boy reformers are moving ahead with their programs to render boys less objectionable, less competitive, more emotionally expressive—more like girls.

Carol Gilligan and her associates are looking for ways to interest boys in gentle nurturing games. She and her associate Elizabeth Debold recently reported finding that 3- and 4-year-old boys "are comfortable playing house or dress up with girls, and assuming nurturing roles in play . . ." They expressed their disappointment that society rarely encourages or sustains the boys' interest in such activities. "By kindergarten, peer socialization and media images kick in."

Inspired by Gilligan, gender educators around the country are now doing their best to interest boys in dolls. This past January, my assistant Elizabeth Bowen attended a conference at Wellesley College for Research on Women that offered a special workshop, "Dolls, Gender and Make-Believe in the Early Childhood Classroom." The Wellesley College scholars were full of ideas on how to re-socialize young males away from competitive play and toward nurturing doll activity.

In July, I attended the 19th annual conference for the National Coalition for Sex Equity in Education (NCSEE) (pronounced "nice-ee"). NCSEE is the professional organization of some six hundred "sex equity experts," most of whom work in the federal government, in state Departments of Education, and in local schools. Gloria Steinem once said, "We need to raise boys like we raise girls," and the NCSEE members are working hard to put Steinem's idea into practice. NCSEE members consider re-socializing boys to be a matter of urgency. I learned at the conference that many of these "equity experts" believe that the schoolyard is a training ground for domestic battery. One keynote speaker identified young male chasing behavior as conducive to future violence. The Wellesley Center, in conjunction with the National Education Association and the Department of Education, has produced a new teacher's guide called *Quit It!* that offers exercises on how to cope with such things as the game of tag and other games involving chasing (p. 86): "Before going outside to play, talk about how students feel when playing a game of tag. Do they like to be chased?

Do they like to do the chasing? How does it feel to be tagged out? Get their ideas about other ways the game might be played. Then, then tell them that they are going to be playing a different kinds of tag, one where nobody is ever 'out'." The guide recommends and gives the rules for new, non-violent, non-competitive version of tag called "Circle of Friends."

Once again, I find that I disagree with what the boy reformers are saying about boys, and I very much object to what they are doing. Frankly, I find some of these gender experts to be more than a little aggressive themselves: with their quilts, and dollhouses, and games like "Circle of Friends." Do they respect boys? Do they even like them?

It never occurs to the would-be reformers of boys that their efforts to overhaul them may be grossly unfair to them. Boys do need to be civilized. They very much need discipline, they need to develop ethical characters: but what they do not need is to be feminized. It is true that boys tend to be less emotionally expressive than girls. But that is a not a psychological or a moral failing.

Boys and girls have different styles of play. Boys, on average, are more active. They are drawn to dynamic outdoor competitive play—with clearly defined winners and losers. At all ages, they take more risks and sustain more injuries than girls. Boys support a multimillion-dollar industry of video and interactive computer games: the goal of most of the games, as one father put it, is to "gain all power, and then destroy the universe." Toy manufactures have never been able to interest many girls in such games.

For years, Mattel looked for ways to market software to girls. During the 1997 Christmas season, they finally broke through to the girl market with two new games: "Barbie Fashion Designer" and then "Talk with me, Barbie." In the latter game, Barbie develops a personal relationship with the girl—learning her name and chatting about dating, careers, and playing house.

Males, young and old, are less interested than females in talking about feelings and personal relationships. But there is no evidence that this is due to oppressive gender stereotypes. On the contrary, the different interests and preferences appear to be hardwired—innate, spontaneously manifested, and probably ineradicable. Gilligan and other feminists talk of a female ethic, an ethic of care, suggesting that girls are morally better, more caring than boys. But no one has been able to show that little girls are nicer or more virtuous than little boys.

It is of course true that boys are more violent than girls. Bullying is a problem in many schools. Boys, being stronger and generally more physically aggressive, do most of the physical bullying, but they do not have a monopoly on malice. Girls are proficient at what sociologists call "relational aggression." They hurt others by shunning, excluding, spreading rumors. Almost any junior high school girl will tell you that girls can create as much misery as boys, especially to other girls.

I see no evidence that boys are morally inferior to girls. They are more reticent about discussing their feelings than girls. But this is not any kind of personality deficit. On the contrary, the reticence may actually be a virtue and a sign of psychological health.

Pollack and his staff at McLean and Gilligan and her colleagues at Harvard are now trying to initiate a national effort to "reconnect boys," to open them up emotionally. Pollack warns parents not be encourage boys to be stoical and silent:

The boy is often pushed to "act like a man," to be the one who is confident and unflinching. No boy should be called upon to be the tough one. No boy should be harmed in this way.

But Pollack needs to show, not merely assume, that it harms a child to be "called upon to be tough." All of the world's major religions place stoical control of emotions at the center of their moral teachings. For Buddhists, the ideal is emotional detachment, for Confucianism, dispassionate control. Christianity enjoins awareness of others' needs and feelings—not your own.

Pollack and Gilligan assume, but never bother to demonstrate, that being emotionally "open" is really such a good thing. That needs to be shown, not assumed. Several recent studies suggest that this popular assumption is quite simply false. I shall be happy to tell you about this research in the question period. But for now, it is enough to say that many psychologists are now suddenly quite skeptical about the value of emotional expressionism.

Moral philosophers and theologians have never believed in emotional expressionism as something to strive for. It's not as if "Be in touch with your feelings" was one of the Ten Commandments. Compared to other cultures (including our own until fairly recent times), contemporary American youth are already far too self-involved and emotionally expressive. The reform-minded experts might even want to consider the possibility that American children may need less, not more, self-involvement. Not only may it be true that American boys don't need to show more emotion, it may also be true that American girls need to be less sentimental and self-absorbed. Maybe all the crashing selves that Pipher talks about are selves that are too self-preoccupied, to the unhealthy exclusion of outside interests.

Children need to be moral more than they need to be in touch with their feelings. They need to have a strong sense of personal responsibility and clear ideas of what is right and wrong. Children do not need feel-good support groups or 12-step programs. Above all, children don't need to have their femininity or masculinity "recreated" or "reconstructed," to use the boy reformers' favorite word.

Aristotle laid down what children *do* need almost 2,500 years ago—clear guidance on how to be moral human beings. What Aristotle advocated became the default mode of moral education over the centuries. And it worked. It is only very recently that many educators began to scorn it.

A society that forsakes its traditional and proven modes of civilizing and humanizing its male children inevitably fails them in fundamental ways. The social costs are considerable since boys who are morally neglected have unpleasant ways of getting themselves noticed. But the greater cost is to the boys themselves. Boys badly need clear, unequivocal rules. They need boundaries. They need structure. Young men have a deep psychological need for honor. To get that need satisfied, they need "directive moral education," explicit instruction from the adults in their lives.

In this final section of my lecture, I want to speak of one area where I believe boys really are in trouble. It has nothing to do with their being pathological, insensitive, or morally shallow; it has to do with the fact that academically, they are doing far worse than girls. This is a genuine problem. Indeed, it is a problem that could become critical. Data from the United States Department of Education, along with several new university studies, show unequivocally that boys are on the weak side of a widening educational gender gap. They are less committed to school than girls, they get lower grades, they are more likely to drop out and to be held back. They are a full year and a half behind girls in their reading and writing skills. They are less likely to go to college: the country's current college freshmen class is 56 percent female, 44 percent male. The enrollment of African-Americans in college is 64 percent female, 36 percent male.

American boys are seriously lagging behind the girls and it keeps getting worse. Bereft of discipline, competitive structures, and direct moral guidance on how to compete and succeed, many American boys do behave badly. They also fare badly academically. The therapeutic pedagogy aggravates that condition. By emphasizing an ethic of feeling over a traditional ethic of right and wrong, by depriving boys of the traditional, effective, time-tested classroom discipline, modern educators are gravely harming boys.

The British know all about this. They are a full five years ahead of us in recognizing the achievement gap between boys and girls and in taking active measures to deal with it. Five years ago British newspapers and journals began telling their readers about the distressing educational deficits of British schoolboys. Reporting that 14-year-old British boys are "on average, more than three years behind girls in English," the *Times* warned of the prospect of "an underclass of permanently unemployed, unskilled men." The *Glasgow Herald* warned: "The gender gap [favoring girls] threatens to become a chasm." The *Economist* referred to boys as "tomorrow's second sex."

In Britain, the public, the government, and the education establishment are focused on the plight of boys. It's a matter of grave public concern. And more and more parents, teachers, and education experts are coming to the conclusion that progressive/therapeutic education does not work for boys. The British are experimenting by bringing back the old-fashioned pedagogies.

The *Daily Telegraph* writer Janet Daly sums up the growing consensus in Britain in a recent talk she gave to the Independent Women's Forum this past September. Referring to the "feminized curriculum," she says:

The consequences have been disastrous for boys, who it turned out, were temperamentally much more dependent than girls on the principles of traditional education: discipline, structure, and competition.

Estelle Morris, a Labour MP who speaks for her party on the subject of education, said, "If we do not start to address the problem young men are facing, we have no hope." Citing many secondary schools who have "identified the difficulties boys experience as a priority" she pointed out that some had begun "implementing successful strategies for raising boys' achievements and expectations." What are some of these strategies?

The principal of the King School was so concerned about the low performance of his boys that he formed a boys-only remedial English class—and brought back practices that had not been seen since the mid-sixties. Here is how one journalist describes a King School class:

Ranks of boys in blazers face the front, giving full attention to the young [male] teacher's instructions. His style is uncompromising and inspirational: "People think that boys like you won't be able to understand writers such as the Romantic poets. Well we're going to prove them wrong. Do you understand?"

According to the reporter, "The class is didactic. Teacher-fronted. Discipline is clear-cut. If homework is not presented, it is completed in detention. No discussion."

This past January, Stephen Byers, school standards minister and a member of the British government, called for a return to traditional structured phonics for teaching reading. He said, "a return to more structured reading lessons will benefit both boys and girls, but the evidence show that it is boys who have been most disadvantaged by the move away from phonics."

The British are allowing stereotypes in the textbooks—it turns out boys enjoy and will read adventure stories with male heroes. War poetry is back.

By contrast with Britain, the American public is not aware that our boys are languishing academically. Our government and education establishment is doing nothing to deal with the ever-widening gender gap that threatens the future of millions of American boys.

How are we to account for this contrast between the U.S. and Britain? What has rendered us so benighted and them so enlightened? The short and accurate answer is that Britain has no Carol Gilligan, no William Pollack or Mary Pipher, no National Coalition of Sex Equity Experts, no Wellesley Center for Research on Women, and no AAUW spreading misinformation about the nation's girls and boys.

In this country, the alarms raised over the shortchanged girls have left no room for concern about the academic deficits of American boys. And today, we find the same forces that promoted the girl-crisis are promoting a boy-crisis. Not about their serious academic deficits but about the boys' "inner child" and their need to be "in touch with their more feminine side." The British public has not been subjected to these harmful distractions.

British parents are demanding more Mrs. Doughertys and fewer Ms. Logans—and they appear to be getting their way. The mood in England is constructive and pragmatic and informed with common sense. The mood here is contentious and ideological and informed with psychobabble. No wonder our public is bewildered and unenlightened about where the boys are.

What we learn from the British is that good information and good social science lead to good educational policy. We need to follow their lead. We're five years behind. It's late, but it's not too late.

Christina Hoff Sommers is an associate professor of philosophy at Clark University.

Reading 5
RACISM AND SEXISM
Paula S. Rothenberg

This is one of the most popular college texts dealing with the issues of racism and sexism in America. This selection is a perfect illustration of the actual attitudes of the politically correct. The assumptions made explicit here are held and preached by the politically correct. Some professors are more, and some are less, explicit when they teach. The basic assumptions are constant. These assumptions are that racism, sexism, and many other forms of bigotry pervade Western culture in general and American culture in particular, that they are learned at an early age and reinforced by a variety of institutions, and that they will continue until the politically correct are triumphant.

* * *

. . . racism and sexism share the following common elements:

1. *Racism involves the subordination of people of color by white people.* While an individual person of color may discriminate against white people or even hate them, his or her behavior or attitude cannot be called "racist". He or she may be considered *prejudiced* against whites and we may all agree that the person acts unfairly and unjustly, but *racism* requires something more than anger, hatred, or prejudice; at the very least, it requires *prejudice plus power*. The history of the

world provides us with a long record of white people holding power and using it to maintain that power and privilege over people of color, not the reverse.

2. *Sexism involves the subordination* of *women by men.* The reasoning here is fairly similar. While some women may dislike men intensely and treat them unfairly and while some women may be equally guilty of prejudice toward other women, the balance of power throughout most, if not all, of recorded history has allowed men to subordinate women in order to maintain their own privilege. Thus, an individual woman who treats men or women unfairly simply because of their gender may be called *prejudiced* and may be criticized as unjust, but she cannot be guilty of sexism. Of course, it is possible to imagine what it would mean for women to be guilty of sexism (or for people of color to be guilty of racism). If a reversal of power should come about so that women and people of color somehow gain fairly comprehensive control of the institutions and ideas of society *and* use them to subordinate men and whites, respectively, we will alter our usage accordingly.

3. *Racism and sexism can be either conscious or unconscious, intentional or unintentional.* Richard Wright describes growing up in the South during the early part of this century and provides us with excellent examples of the kind of blatant, conscious, intentional racism that most of us take as stereotypical. However, once we proceed to the fourth selection, the job of definition becomes more difficult. "'Bias Incident' at Staten Island's Miller Field" presents a disturbing example of racism carried out by a group of people who staunchly affirm, "We're not racists." Why do these people maintain this innocence in light of the incident described? What does their insistence tell us about racism? One lesson to be learned is that it is possible for a person to believe passionately that he or she is not racist or sexist but to be mistaken. Along these same lines, "Hidden Lessons" takes our inquiry further into the unconscious nature of racism and sexism by showing us how even teachers firmly committed to treating boy and girl students "equally" may themselves, unconsciously, and unintentionally, be guilty of sexism . . .

Paula S. Rothenberg is a professor at William Paterson University in New Jersey.

Reading 6
APOLOGIZE FOR BEING HETEROSEXUAL

At most colleges there is an emphasis on indoctrinating the students into accepting the politically correct worldview as the only way for a good person to view the world. The effort is especially intense regarding the student managers (resident assistants) in the dormitories. At many schools potential student assistants are required to make judgments regarding skits or movies, which involve dealing with groups deemed by the politically correct to be oppressed. Those who fail to show politically correct attitudes are not hired.

In these "sensitivity" or "struggle" sessions, students are urged to engage in public confessions of their "sins". Almost everyone has to confess because just belonging to an "oppressor" group is considered a sin in itself. Although the list may vary, it usually includes all white people and all males in general, as well as heterosexuals, people born in middle-class families, capitalists, businessmen, and husbands. The following is an apology that must be stated or signed by people who are in officially designated "privilege" categories, such as heterosexuals. Once you have been through the training and confessed your sins, you are considered to be on your way to having your "consciousness raised." This means you see the truth according to the PC. Only after this can you find redemption. The PC form a kind of church so it is only reasonable that they have rituals that resemble other religions, in this case dealing with sin and redemption. The following is a typical "confession" and is part of a PC handbook used to train students to be assistant managers of dormitories.

WORKING WITH GAY, LESBIAN, AND BISEXUAL STUDENTS IN THE RESIDENCE HALLS

I, _____, understand that it is ok to be imperfect with regards to homophobia and heterosexism. It is ok if I do not know all of the answers or if at times my ignorance and misunderstandings become obvious.

I have permission to ask questions that appear stupid.

I have permission to struggle with these issues and be up-front and honest about my feelings.

I am a product of a homophobic and heterosexist culture, and I am who I am. I don't have to feel guilty about what I know or believe, but I do need to take responsibility for what I can do now: trying to learn as much as I can struggling to change my false and inaccurate beliefs and oppressive attitudes and actions.

Reading 7
WHAT IS LOST WITH A POLITICALLY CORRECT EDUCATION?
George Zilbergeld

To most people who do not work in a university, the culture wars being waged on campuses must seem the very essence of "ignorant armies clashing at night." If the issue crosses the radar screen of people at all, it probably only causes them to wonder how there can be adults who have the energy to argue over such matters after a hard day's work. However, the culture wars are having a profound and damaging effect on this country. The politically correct education that all too many students are receiving undermines the major goals of a college education that are critical to the future of the students and of the country.

Three of the major reasons a person acquires a college education are to prepare for a career, to better understand oneself, and to become a knowledgeable citizen. The ideology of political correctness, which is based on the notion that there is no objective view of the world even in the sciences, but only a variety of "stories" conditioned by one's race, class, and gender, leads to an educational approach that thwarts the development of the skills that are essential to accomplishing all of these goals.

One of the primary reasons students seek a college education is to prepare for a career in which they can use more of their intelligence and less of their muscles. Many studies and common sense have shown that certain skills never go out of style. The ability to write clearly, to read critically, and to do basic research will always be needed. A major problem with a politically correct education is that time that could be spent acquiring these skills is spent learning a new ideology and a strange vocabulary.

For example, instead of analyzing texts, students are told to "deconstruct" them. The PC vocabulary often strikes people as a kind of secret decoder-ring language, previously reserved for nine-year-old boys, now used by tenured professors. An entire time-consuming PC vocabulary, including such terms as empowerment, hegemony, and institutional racism must be mastered. Unfortunately this ideological self-indulgence hurts the least well prepared the most. A middle-class student can live off the vocabulary he learned from his family and twelve years in a good suburban school system. College students who learned less at home and attended poorer schools may be denied the opportunity to learn the real vocabulary that grown-ups use in business, law, or medicine. Because acquiring a new ideology involves so much unlearning and relearning and reinforcement, it takes a lot of time, time that must be taken away from learning how to read, write, and understand such subjects as calculus and chemistry.

One essential skill students should learn in college is that of expressing themselves clearly in writing. The apostles of PC teach exactly the opposite, providing remarkable examples of opaque writing. Here is Professor Frederic Jameson explaining goodness-knows-what in his book *Signatures of the Visible:*

The visual is essentially pornographic, which is to say that it has its end in rapt, mindless fascination; thinking about its attributes becomes an adjunct to that, if it is unwilling to betray its object; while that most austere films necessarily draw their energy from the attempt to repress their energy from the attempt to repress their own excess (rather than from the more thankless effort to discipline the viewer).

It would be a mistake to think that this is an isolated horror story. Here is another example by Jacques Derrida, father of deconstructionism and one of the leaders of the movement to substitute race, class, and gender analysis for other means of analyzing literature:

A written sign is proffered in the absence of the receiver. How to style this absence? One could say at the moment when I am writing, the receiver may be absent from my field of present perception. But is not this absence merely a distant presence, or which, in one form or another, is idealized in its representation? This does not seem to be the case, or at least this distance, divergence, delay, this deferral must be capable of being carried to a certain absoluteness of absence if the structure of writing, assuming that writing exists, is to constitute itself. It is at that point that the difference as writing could no longer be an ontological modification of presence.

In what field of endeavor would this style of writing prove useful? Would you want these folks to write the instructions for your open-heart surgery? Would you like one of their students to write an instruction manual for the use of heavy electrical equipment? If clear writing is clear thinking, what does this say about the thought processes characteristic of the PC movement? If anyone thinks these are exceptional examples, I suggest he sample the writings of the politically correct and experience for himself the prevalence of this type of expression. In undergraduate school students either will or won't learn many of the skills they need for the rest of their lives. Students are being cheated if they aren't learning basic skills in college. It is possible that if one attends a very prestigious school, he can get by with just the name. For everyone else it is going to be rough sledding if they lack the basic skills.

Not only is much time spent trying to reprogram undergraduates to use an obscure and unnatural language, but attitudes taught in PC classes will be derided in any corporate setting. Imagine saying in a crisis meeting over corporate strategy that it doesn't matter what the corporation does because "there is no knowledge, no standard, no choice that is objective" (Barbara Hernstein-Smith, professor of English at Duke University). Does she mean that it doesn't matter where the surgeon cuts, or how much steel is used in the suspension bridge?

Another basic skill students should learn in college is the ability to do objective research. Some aspects of basic research include being able to locate important facts and statistics, knowing how to form and test hypotheses, and being familiar with the views of people who disagree with you. A PC education underrates and undermines all of these skills. The politically correct seldom encourage the habit of looking up facts because facts may be at odds with ideology. One of the main tenets of the PC crowd is that we don't spend enough money helping people in need. Perhaps. If a student mentions a topic such as food stamps, I always say, "Lets get the facts. How much do you think we do spend on food stamps?" I then point out that it is often very easy to find the facts. Any yearly Almanac will have a basic copy of the federal budget. When students see that we spend $20 billion each year they are often surprised. When I ask why, they say that they had never looked at the actual number because they thought only specialists could get that information, or because other professors had convinced them that there was no need—that everyone already "knew" that we weren't spending very much for the poor.

Before the anniversary of the bombing of Hiroshima, I ask students to watch the national network coverage. ABC is especially good because it nearly always has extensive coverage, including pictures of the horribly wounded and the number of Japanese killed. I then ask the students how many Japanese were killed and how many people the Japanese killed during World War II. Students often struggle with how to find the total number of those killed by the Japanese. I point out that they can obtain that number by just adding up the number killed in each of the countries conquered by the Japanese during World War II. Students are invariably surprised that the number killed in China alone is over ten million, while the number of Japanese killed during the entire war is under three million. Looking at the facts makes it a good deal harder to portray the United States as uniquely evil because it used the atomic bomb.

Understanding the techniques of comparative analysis is an essential tool of basic research. In the social sciences, comparative analysis often provides a substitute for the kind of controlled experiments that can be performed in the natural sciences. Comparative analysis of social situations involves the following steps: Form a hypothesis about how the world works, and then look at various times and places to see if your hypothesis holds up. For example, you might form the hypothesis that crowding causes people to become angry more often and commit more crimes than those who have more space. You could then look at nations throughout the world and compare population density figures against crime rates.

Of course obtaining conclusive results can be a very sophisticated undertaking. But an initial analysis would immediately indicate some problems with the hypothesis. Some of the most crowded countries, such as Japan, Holland, and Singapore, turn out to have some of the lowest crime rates in the world. This method will seldom be taught by the politically correct because objective comparative analysis will often cast doubt upon their simplistic ideological analyses.

You can still argue that we should spend more for food stamps. But now you are arguing using facts, something often appreciated outside of universities. It is easier to make the claim that this country doesn't care about the poor if you don't add up the numbers. Then you won't know that we spend $20 billion on the food stamp program every year or that the average American Indian family of four receives $20,000 per year from the federal government. Most students who look at the actual numbers are surprised that the difference between the rates of black and white poverty are not greater than they are, although any difference is deplorable. Crime statistics, especially those involving hate crimes, are even more of a revelation. Students are often surprised to learn that whites are much less likely to commit violent crimes against blacks than blacks are against whites and that members of minority groups commit a substantial number of hate crimes.

A third aspect of responsible research and critical thinking is to learn what opponents of your point of view have to say. Reading another point of view is always difficult because we all become too comfortable with our own viewpoints. Liberals read the *New York Times* and conservatives, the *Wall Street Journal*. Good teachers should encourage students to read both. This habit of examining both sides is unlikely to be cultivated as part of a politically correct education because the politically correct are so convinced that they have a monopoly on the truth. The politically correct are in a position similar to that of the communists who always had to worry that people would see or read another point of view and then ask inconvenient questions.

Because the PC movement concentrates so heavily on race, class, and gender analysis, entire sections of the world disappear. An area that they hardly ever mention, except in a derisive way, is that of small business. Yet the facts are clear. There is probably no better way for an entire group of people to raise themselves to middle class status in a single generation than by owning their own small businesses. PC professors who say they care about underprivileged minorities don't mention that, historically, groups that emphasize politics as their main strategy for improving their position take a long time to climb the economic ladder, while groups that emphasize owning businesses have done much better. But the politically correct don't like capitalism. They don't like business people, who appear only as exploiters in their worldview. They don't like to praise the virtues, such as courage, persistence, and endless hard work, needed to succeed in a small business. Thus they may discourage many of their students from pursuing some of their best opportunities.

While it may not be the main reason students go to college, most people would agree that gaining a deeper understanding of oneself is a legitimate and important goal of a college education. For thousands of years, people have agreed with Socrates that the examined life is superior to the unexamined life. One of the best ways of examining one's life is through the use of imaginative literature such as poetry, drama, and novels. For this reason it is hard to imagine a college that does not include this material in its curriculum. All colleges still list such courses in their catalogs and curricula. However, in an increasing number of colleges, courses in the great imaginative literature of such authors as Shakespeare or Keats is no longer required, even for English majors. Even when such courses are offered, they often focus on the race, class, and gender prejudices of the author and his times, to the exclusion of what these great authors might have to teach us. What could be a genuinely broadening experience, helping us reflect on our own experiences and transporting us beyond the limitations of our own experience, is instead reduced to an endless bitter analysis of which groups are the oppressors and which the oppressed.

Certainly some of who we are reflects our race, class, and gender. But how much more of who we are is a reflection of universal human experiences and dilemmas? The politically correct believe that issues of race, class, and gender are the main stumbling blocks to human happiness and that those people who are white, western, male, and middle-class are uniquely evil and responsible for the evils of this world. Thus PC professors who do use texts by dead white males insist on a pound of interpretation for every ounce of text, lest the flock of students go astray.

When such professors teach Shakespeare, they often use his plays primarily to illustrate the evils of white men. Does this really benefit students, or would they be better off meeting these great writers on their own terms? Is an increased ability to perform race, class, and gender analysis a worthwhile substitute for gaining enough knowledge of imaginative literature to reflect more deeply on our own experience as we confront such issues as love and hate, loneliness and friendship, and death and loss.

Thus to teach material written by these folks, without emphasizing their biases, only adds to human unhappiness. Shakespeare, for example, is taught in fewer and fewer schools and is not even required for all English majors. Is time taking Shakespeare seriously well spent, or would the time be better spent on questions of race, class, and gender? When you have trouble speaking to someone you love, and it reminds you of how Cordelia in King Lear once lamented that "I cannot heave my heart in to my mouth", and that you had better learn how to do so or you might bring about a sad ending as well, isn't that time well spent? Or will it mean more to know that you once had a teacher who said that the real problem in King Lear is the patriarchal system?

When you are caught between following custom or getting your heart's desire, will you be pleased to wonder if, like Edmund the bastard son of Gloucester, you should allow the "plague of custom" to deprive you of what you want, or you should decide to shout, "Now, gods, stand up for bastards" and go after what you want in the same ruthless way as did Edmund? Will you be pleased, if when you are feeling the pain of the loss of a loved one, you can recall how a poet felt after the loss of his child that he "had lost the best part of me"? Or will it provide more solace to recall that the poet was white and male? In a bitter moment will you be more likely to be angry regarding race, class, and gender issues, or will you wonder if your epitaph will be that "Life was not gentle to him,/And the elements so mixed in him/That he made warfare on life,/In which he was slain" (*Spoon River Anthology*).

Will it matter that you can use the literature of your college years to reflect on our own happiness or sadness, or do you think that the important experiences of your life will revolve around race, class, and gender problems? Will your heart recall a young love as someone "who walks in beauty" or will you stir with the knowledge of her damn middle-class values and refusal to acknowledge the sins of the white man? How much is lost if a student doesn't have the opportunity of reading about the sadness of getting old by reading Yeats' "There is No Country for Old People"? How much is lost if you don't know that Yeats is a white male.

Is it really believable that the plays, poems, and novels by people like Shakespeare, Blake, and Dickens have only lasted because of a universal plot by white men or is it because they speak about eternal parts of human experience in ways that matter?

One of the major issues connected with self-knowledge that is currently getting a lot of attention is the issue of the role of education in building self-esteem. A good education builds the confidence and self-esteem of all students based on their real accomplishments. Many of the PC believe that everyone's self-esteem should be raised regardless of actual accomplishments, since criteria used to measure excellence are culturally biased and should not be taken seriously as an objective measures of accomplishments.

They believe that the best way to increase the confidence and performance of minority students is to emphasize the past accomplishments of members of these groups, which may previously have been neglected due to habit or discrimination. Thus PC education concentrates on raising the confidence level of government-preferred minority groups by insuring that the accomplishments of members of these groups receive as much attention as those of dead white males.

The nonpolitically correct view is that real self-confidence comes only from real accomplishments. Knowing about one's ancestors' accomplishments may be encouraging, but only one's own accomplishments build genuine self-esteem.

Is self-esteem a by-product of having confidence in one's ability to do things that are considered important in today's society, such as writing well, analyzing difficult material, and understanding algebra, or is self-esteem a by-product of being told that your ancestors played a more significant role in history than was previously thought? Is it possible that the Asian Americans are wrong when they concentrate on subjects like calculus and chemistry? Would most Japanese Americans, feel better about themselves and accomplish more if they stopped taking all those math and science courses and started delving more deeply into the history of Japan and its accomplishments? Do the Asian Americans seem to lack self-esteem because they lack detailed information on the history of Japan, China, India, and Korea?

While a PC education may not help self-esteem, it certainly has an effect on the level of anger. Many PC professors don't seem to understand what has happened because they get the "right answers" back on examinations and during class discussions. For some reason the PC professors don't seem to take into account the possibility that the students don't like having their white, middle-class parents and grandparents insulted and that the students think the United States is a fine place to live.

There is only a limited amount of classroom time. Should professors spend their time teaching students to write well, analyze difficult material, and learn research skills or attempting to raise the self-esteem of students? A choice must be made. If you don't enter into the discussion then the decision will be made by the most focused and relentless of the groups—and so far that has been the politically correct. Do you like the results so far?

Should the politically correct press on with your blessing? Should the government-preferred minority groups concentrate on raising their self-esteem now and get their basic reading, writing, and math skills later on when the time is ripe for such an effort? Or will the whites and Asians be so far ahead in skills (although possibly nowhere near as full of self-esteem) that they won't even know in what direction to look for the government-preferred minorities who have been left behind?

One of the prime ways to develop real self-esteem is to have the opportunity to express one's opinion in a supportive atmosphere. The appropriate combination of support and resistance is what the best parents and professors do for their students. But the politically correct are more like a group of religious zealots than teachers.

Since they are absolutely convinced that their way is the only way it is very hard for them to allow a truly open debate. Students in classes taught by these fanatics spend too much of their time trying to figure out exactly what ideology is desired and too little time thinking about the issues. These are definitely not safe places to think in an open manner. You risk ridicule and poor grades. That is too much of a risk for practically all undergraduates. Besides, no one is quicker to figure out what is selling than undergraduates.

As education has become available for more and more people, it has led to more equal learning opportunities and thus allowed people to feel that they are on an equal plane with other students even if their schools are not as prestigious. Thus anyone who reads Tolstoy or Shakespeare might be considered to be on fairly equal ground with anyone else who has read the same material. Knowing that you have read Shakespeare or the *Federalist Papers,* and not just someone else's analysis about them, provides a quiet confidence and a feeling of well-being that you have the basic building blocks that allow you to make independent and worthwhile judgments. After all, who can read better material? Reading the classics provides feelings of real confidence and equality. Reading the politically correct material makes you into a novice again. You are always less than those who have the secret knowledge. And if, as has happened with so much of Marxism, it all turns out to be a fad that fails, you are left with nothing at all.

A third benefit of college education is to become a knowledgeable citizen. Often the skills needed for a successful career are the same skills and attitudes needed to be an intelligent and independently thinking citizen. Knowing that basic statistics are available on just about any subject is a vital skill. Just knowing that a single volume, *The Statistical Abstract of the United States*, is the single best source of statistics on domestic matters is helpful. Confidence is gained by having looked up information often enough so that one is not intimidated when a new search is needed. Skills such as the habit and ability to quickly find factual information are of obvious value here as well. In addition, citizenship also depends on judgment developed by such means as reading history. The politically correct can never allow an open reading of history for the same reason that they don't want to encourage people to look up facts on their own, do comparative analysis, or read a different point of view. It lessens their authority and could destroy their credibility.

Students who have received a PC education have learned all about America's defects and mistakes, but little about its virtues and accomplishments. I have students nowadays who are very knowledgeable about the relocation camps where the Japanese Americans were kept during World War II. Some even make comparisons between these relocation camps and Nazi concentration camps. If I ask if they have seen photographs, they often say no. If I ask if they saw pictures of the women in the beauty parlor, they stare in disbelief. I bring in the photographs that show scenes of everyday life, such as the beauty parlor, and ask if they think that there were beauty parlor rooms in the German concentration camps. The students often ask where I got such photographs—if I have a special source. When I point out that these photographs are readily available in such collections as *Life Goes to War*, they are shocked. While all agree that the imprisonment of the Japanese Americans is a terrible wrong, they also are surprised about the conditions of the prisons. If I ask how many Japanese Americans were killed by the United States government, they don't know. The answer is one. If I ask how many Jews were murdered in Auschwitz in a single day and provide the answer (about 4000) they quickly begin to wonder about the reliability of the professor who told them that we had concentration camps in America.

If professors want to see the power of knowing history, they might ask students to debate whether we should have dropped the atomic bombs on Hiroshima and Nagasaki. First, ask for a debate without any particular introduction.

This is the usual method of dealing with the sins of the United States—all the details of the horrors are given when it is the United States that has committed the horrors. Read a few pages from *Unit 731*, the story of how Japan used "medical experiments" on human beings to test biological weapons and how the Japanese regularly practiced vivisection on captured civilians—and then have the debate on whether we should have dropped the atomic bombs on Japan. Of course this doesn't settle the issue, but for many students it does lend some perspective.

How can one be a knowledgeable citizen without a thorough knowledge of the history of the civilization that spawned personal liberty and democracy?

The constant repetition of the idea that white people, the West, and the United States are unique repositories of evil tends to weaken the affection people have for this democracy. How useful is a politically correct version of history that is basically a catalog of the sins of the West and the white man? It is not merely that it is false; it doesn't give you a means of developing your judgment.

A politically correct education also enforces habits that are not good for democracy. An ideological education supports the view of the world in which one's opponents are enemies who must be destroyed, instead of fellow citizens who disagree on a particular issue.

In general the wrong values are taught when ideologues do the teaching. Lying, ignoring inconvenient facts, and keeping silent or condoning uncivil behavior when the people using such language are your ideological friends is exactly what the politically correct do on a regular basis. Professors and colleges teach by example. Today what they often teach is that lying with a straight face is just fine. After all, how many colleges state that they don't discriminate when that is exactly what they do in admissions, financial aid, and hiring?

Students who attend college today will be citizens who will not gain a true picture of the world. Entire parts of history and society are ignored. Only the negative aspects of the West and the United States are examined in detail. Students who only had information from PC professors would be hard pressed to explain why people from all over the world want to come to America.

The importance of military valor to the maintenance of a free society is never discussed. Without real knowledge about war, it will be hard to have a feel for what happens when a country goes to war unprepared in material, training, and spirit. How can citizens make a rational choice between unnecessary wars and wars that should be fought and expenditures that must be made, unless they are given a chance to see all sides of the arguments regarding war? The lack of attention paid to military matters created the ludicrous situation in which so many professors predicted disaster for the U.S. before the Gulf War.

Professors who have never been in the military, let alone a war, and who had no idea of the nature of modern warfare, sounded so confident before the war and were so silent after the four-day victory that you would think that it would shut them up for a long time. You would be wrong. How fortunate for them that their mistakes are forgotten every four years as each cohort of students graduates.

For the sake of self-development, our careers and our children's careers, and for the sake of our country, a politically correct education seems like a very poor choice.

2

The Environmental Movement: Separating Science and Ideology

During the past twenty-five years, an increasing number of people have become aware of the threats to the environment and the need to protect nature. At this time it would be hard to find many people in the United States who do not care about the environment. The PC movement has used legitimate concerns regarding the environment to attack free enterprise, the government, and even science. In doing so the PC movement has corrupted not only the social sciences and the humanities, but even the physical sciences. In addition, an important wing of the environmental movement appears to hate not just science but much of the modern world. They often depict human beings as a malevolent force in contrast to the good and pure natural world. The articles in this chapter are meant to provide some balance in our view of nature.

In "Social Dogmas and Pseudoscience," Thomas Sowell attacks the use of what he calls "junk science" by intellectuals on the left to promote ideas that don't have any real scientific basis. He argues that they distort what modern science teaches us about that importance of the position of the observer to create support for a broader moral and cultural relativism.

Julian Simon, in "More People, Greater Wealth," shows that many of our worries about running out of resources are unfounded. We have been so inundated by the view that everything in the environment is getting worse that Simon's views seem counterintuitive. Most people are convinced that we are running out of essential natural resources. But if you ask people to name examples, most will be stymied. Furthermore, they will find it hard to name a single natural resource that we have run out of over the last hundred years without coming up with a satisfactory substitute.

Extremists in the environmental movement have sought to demonize anyone who protests that a particular scare is not based on strong scientific evidence. It seems that not a month goes by without a new health scare. Scares often exert considerable influence even in the absence of hard science. The media, especially television, seems to have a much greater effect than the views of scientists. When Meryl Streep, actress and part-time toxicologist, testified before a congressional committee on the danger of Alar, a spray used to protect apples, it was immediately withdrawn from use. The only known result was to bankrupt a number of small apple farmers. In "Facts versus Fears," The American Council of Science and Health documents a number of examples in which fear has won out over science.

Although the PC profess a great love of people in third world countries, some writers such as Steve Milloy, in "DDT is Genocidal," point out that the views of the PC often have a detrimental effect on the poorest of the poor and that, with the PC, ideology comes before people. It seems that the PC are most dedicated to helping people they don't actually know. Like the Russian landowner who finds the living men and women that he knows to be unworthy of his attention, and then decides to dedicate himself "to the service of mankind," the PC often seem to love those they know the least.

For many years, much of the intellectual establishment has had an antagonistic view toward modern technology. Perhaps it offers them a way to feel superior to most Americans, who love their cars, electric toothbrushes, and television. Why do so many take such pride in saying that *they* never watch that "vast wasteland," television, and in condemning the spending habits of most Americans? No part of modern technology has earned more opprobrium than the automobile. There is something about cars in particular that drives the average intellectual wild. There are many good reasons to dislike cars, but do any of them explain the fury and disdain cars arouse? Why do so many preach the virtues of mass transit while continuing to drive their own cars whenever possible? James Q. Wilson addresses these and other questions in his provocative "Cars and Their Enemies."

Reading 8
SOCIAL DOGMAS AND PSEUDOSCIENCE
Thomas Sowell

The junk science that has become one of the hallmarks of the crusades of the political left, both in and out of the courtroom, has a long pedigree. The left has for centuries tried to use the mystique of science to promote ideas that not only have no scientific basis, but are often the very antithesis of science.

In the 19th century, Marx and Engels referred to their social dogmas as "scientific socialism." A century earlier, Condorcet analogized social issues to engineering problems. But there was no more relationship between these notions and science or engineering than there is between today's cultural relativism and Einstein's theory of relativity.

Einstein said that the position of the observer is an integral part of the data, but he did not say that it was the only part of the data, as sweeping leftist dismissals of "bourgeois" economics or of the ideas of "dead white males" might suggest. Moreover, the position of the observer was not a merely subjective matter, as you might think from listening to the deconstructionists. Distance, as well as the angle of view, defines the position of the observer in science. We see the moon where it was about a second ago and the sun where it was 8 minutes ago. At night we can see one star where it was more than 20 years ago and another star where it was centuries ago.

Modern science, like ancient philosophy, concludes that appearances can differ greatly from reality, but that is wholly different from saying that there is no reality beyond our subjective perceptions. The very reason complex mathematical calculations are necessary for sending spacecraft to other planets is that, while these planets are not where we see them, there is some objectively determined place where they are now and where they will be when the spacecraft reaches them.

You can't point a rocket at Mars or Neptune and blast off. Even if we did not have to contend with the effects of the spinning of the Earth and other influences on the path of the rocket, the objective positions of Mars and Venus must first be determined. Moreover, those positions can be determined objectively because science is the opposite of subjectivism.

My earliest exposure to the role of the position of the observer came from sitting in the bleachers at Yankee Stadium as a teenager. I was puzzled to see a batter hit the ball and then—perhaps half a second later—hear the crack of the bat. That didn't happen when I was sitting behind home plate. It was a much longer distance to the bleachers, and light and sound travel at very different speeds.

When distances are astronomical, light can take years, centuries or even millennia to reach an observer, destroying the illusion that sight is instantaneous. If beings in some distant galaxy had telescopes powerful enough to see lower Manhattan, they would not see the World Trade Center today.

They would be more likely to see dinosaurs. It would be many centuries from now before they could see the World Trade Center being built.

However radically appearances and reality may differ, there are fixed links between them, and science is the working out of what those links are. Romanticism is the notion that we can take the unreliability of appearances as a license to pretend that reality is whatever we choose to make it. Leftist romanticism is the notion that government can make reality conform to our visions.

Where science and the social visions of the left differ most is in testing their beliefs against empirical evidence. For science, such tests are essential. For the left, evasions of such tests are essential. Those academic fields most subject to empirical verification—physics, engineering, and the like—are the least affected by the leftism that pervades the softer fields. The ability of the left to ignore such evidence as appears spontaneously has been one of the frightening triumphs of the human will. Through most of the 20th century, most Western intellectuals have favored various forms of socialism around the world, despite its record of extraordinary economic failure in democratic countries and brutal slaughters in communist countries.

For decades on end, leftist intellectuals have ignored the refugee flight of millions of people from the lands where the left reigned. Many of the butchers they fled, including Stalin and Mao, were regarded as heroes to the American left. Nothing could so epitomize the difference between science and pseudoscience.

Thomas Sowell is an economist and a senior fellow at the Hoover Institution in Stanford, California.

Reading 9
MORE PEOPLE, GREATER WEALTH, MORE RESOURCES, HEALTHIER ENVIRONMENT
Julian L. Simon

INTRODUCTION

This is the economic history of humanity in a nutshell: From 2 million or 200,000 or 20,000 or 2,000 years ago until the 18th century there was slow growth in population, almost no increase in health or decrease in mortality, slow growth in the availability of natural resources (but not increased scarcity), increase in wealth for a few, and mixed effects on the environment. Since then there has been rapid growth in population due to spectacular decreases in the death rate, rapid growth in resources, widespread increases in wealth, and an unprecedently clean and beautiful living environment in many parts of the world along with a degraded environment in the poor and socialist parts of the world.

That is, more people and more wealth has correlated with more (rather than less) resources and a cleaner environment—just the opposite of what Malthusian theory leads one to believe. The task before us is to make sense of these mind-boggling happy trends.

The current gloom and doom about a "crisis" of our environment is all wrong on the scientific facts. Even the U.S. Environmental Protection Agency acknowledges that U.S. air and water have been getting cleaner rather than dirtier in the past few decades. Every agricultural economist knows that the world's population has been eating ever-better since World War II. Every resource economist knows that all natural resources have been getting more available rather than more scarce, as shown by their falling prices over the decades and centuries. And every demographer knows that the death rate has been falling all over the world, life expectancy almost tripling in the rich countries in the past two centuries, and almost doubling in the poor countries in just the past four decades.

The picture also is now clear that population growth does not hinder economic development. In the 1980s there was a complete reversal in the consensus of thinking of population economists about the effects of more people. In 1986, the National Research Council and the National Academy of Sciences completely overturned its "official" view away from the earlier worried view expressed in 1971. It noted the absence of any statistical evidence of a negative connection between population increase and economic growth. And it said that "The scarcity of exhaustible resources is at most a minor restraint on economic growth."

This U-turn by the scientific consensus of experts on the subject has gone unacknowledged by the press, the anti-natalist environmental organizations, and the agencies that foster population control abroad.

Here is my central assertion: Almost every economic and social change or trend points in a positive direction, as long as we view the matter over a reasonably long period of time.

For proper understanding of the important aspects of an economy we should look at the long-run trends. But the short-run comparisons—between the sexes, age groups, races, political groups, which are usually purely relative—make more news. To repeat, just about every important long-run measure of human welfare shows improvement over the decades and centuries, in the United States as well as in the rest of the world. And there is no persuasive reason to believe that these trends will not continue indefinitely.

Would I bet on it? For sure. I'll bet a week's or month's pay—anything I win goes to pay for more research—that just about any trend pertaining to material human welfare will improve rather than get worse. You pick the comparison and the year.

THE FACTS

Let's quickly review a few data on how human life has been doing, beginning with the all-important issue, life itself.

The Conquest of Too-Early Death

The most important and amazing demographic fact—the greatest human achievement in history, in my view—is the decrease in the world's death rate. Consider the history of human life expectancy at birth. It took thousands of years to increase life expectancy at birth from just over 20 years to the high 20s about 1750. Then about 1750 life expectancy in the richest countries suddenly took off and tripled in about two centuries. In just the past two centuries, the length of life you could expect for your baby or yourself in the advanced countries jumped from less than 30 years to perhaps 75 years. What greater event has humanity witnessed than this conquest of premature death in the rich countries? It is this decrease in the death rate that is the cause of there being a larger world population nowadays than in former times.

Then starting well after World War II, the length of life you could expect in the poor countries has leaped upwards by perhaps fifteen or even twenty years since the 1950s, caused by advances in agriculture, sanitation, and medicine.

Let's put it differently. In the 19th century the planet Earth could sustain only one billion people. Ten thousand years ago, only 4 million could keep themselves alive. Now, 5 billion people are living longer and more healthily than ever before, on average. The increase in the world's population represents our victory over death.

Here arises a crucial issue of interpretation: One would expect lovers of humanity to jump with joy at this triumph of human mind and organization over the raw killing forces of nature. Instead, many lament that there are so many people alive to enjoy the gift of life, even regretting the lower death rate. And it is this worry that leads them to approve the Indonesian, Chinese and other inhumane programs of coercion and denial of personal liberty in one of the most precious choices a family can make—the number of children that it wishes to bear and raise.

The Decreasing Scarcity of Natural Resources

Throughout history, the supply of natural resources always has worried people. Yet the data clearly show that natural resource scarcity—as measured by the economically meaningful indicator of cost or price—has been decreasing rather than increasing in the long run for all raw materials, with only temporary exceptions from time to time. That is, availability has been increasing. Consider copper, which is representative of all the metals. If we look at the price relative to wages since 1801, we see the cost of a ton is only about a tenth now of what it was two hundred years ago.

This trend of falling prices of copper has been going on for a very long time. In the 18th century B.C.E. in Babylonia under Hammurabi—almost 4,000 years ago—the price of copper was about a thousand times its price in the U.S. now relative to wages. At the time of the Roman Empire the price was about a hundred times the present price.

Everything that we buy—pens, shirts, tires—has been getting cheaper over the years because we know how to make them cheaper, especially during the past 200 years. Even so, the extraordinary fact is that natural resources have been getting cheaper even faster than consumer goods. So by any measure, natural resources have been getting more available rather than more scarce.

Regarding oil, the shocking price rises during the 1970s and 1980s were not caused by growing scarcity in the world supply. And indeed, the price of petroleum in inflation-adjusted dollars has returned to levels about where they were before the politically induced increases, and the price of gasoline is about at the historic low and still falling. Concerning energy in general, there is no reason to believe that the supply of energy is finite, or that the price of energy will not continue its long-run decrease forever.

Food is an especially important resource. The evidence is particularly strong for food that we are on a benign trend despite rising population. The long-run price of food relative to wages is now only perhaps a tenth as much as it was in 1800 in the U.S. Even relative to consumer products the price of grain is down, due to increased productivity, just as with all other primary products. Famine deaths due to insufficient food supply have decreased even in absolute terms, let alone relative to population, in the past century, a matter which pertains particularly to the poor countries. Per-person food consumption is up over the last 30 years. And there are no data showing that the bottom of the income scale is faring worse, or even has failed to share in the general improvement, as the average has improved.

Africa's food production per person is down, but by 1994 almost no one any longer claims that Africa's suffering results from a shortage of land or water or sun. The cause of hunger in Africa is a combination of civil wars and collectivization of agriculture, which periodic droughts have made more murderous.

Consider agricultural land as an example of all natural resources. Though many people consider land to be a special kind of resource, it is subject to the same processes of human creation as other natural resources. The most important fact about agricultural land is that less and less of it is needed as the decades pass. This idea is utterly counter-intuitive. It seems entirely obvious that a growing world population would need larger amounts of farmland. But the title of a remarkable, prescient article in 1951 by Theodore Schultz tells the story: "The Declining Economic Importance of Land."

The increase in actual and potential productivity per unit of land has grown much faster than population, and there is sound reason to expect this trend to continue. Therefore, there is less and less reason to worry about the supply of land. Though the stock of usable land seems fixed at any moment, it is constantly being increased—at a rapid rate in many cases—by the clearing of new land or reclamation of wasteland. Land also is constantly being enhanced by increasing the number of crops grown per year on each unit of land and by increasing the yield per crop with better farming methods and with chemical fertilizer. Last but not least, land is created anew where there was no land.

There is only one important resource that has shown a trend of increasing scarcity rather than increasing abundance. That resource is the most important of all—human beings. Yes, there are more people on earth now than ever before. But if we measure the scarcity of people the same way that we measure the scarcity of other economic goods—by how much we must pay to obtain their services—we see that wages and salaries have been going up all over the world, in poor countries as well as in rich countries. The amount that you must pay to obtain the services of a barber or a cook has risen in India, just as the price of a barber or cook—or economist—has risen in the United States over the decades. This increase in the price of peoples' services is a clear indication that people are becoming scarcer even though there are more of us.

About pollution now: Surveys show that the public believes that our air and water have been getting more polluted in recent years. The evidence with respect to air indicates that pollutants have been declining, especially the main pollutant, particulates. With respect to water, the proportion of monitoring sites in the U.S. with water of good drinkability has increased since the data began in 1961.

Every forecast of the doomsayers has turned out flat wrong. Metals, foods, and other natural resources have become more available rather than scarcer throughout the centuries. The famous Famine 1975 forecast by the Paddock brothers—that we would see millions of famine deaths in the U.S. on television in the 1970s—was followed instead by gluts in agricultural markets. Paul Ehrlich's primal scream about "What will we do when the [gasoline] pumps run dry?" was followed by gasoline cheaper than since the 1930s. The Great Lakes are not dead; instead they offer better sport fishing than ever. The main pollutants, especially the particulates that have killed people for years, have lessened in our cities. (Socialist countries are a different and tragic environmental story, however!)

The wrong forecasts of shortages of copper and other metals have not been harmless, however. They have helped cause economic disasters for mining companies and for the poor countries that depend upon mining, by misleading them with unsound expectations of increased prices. But nothing has reduced the doomsayers' credibility with the press or their command over the funding resources of the federal government.

Let's dramatize these sets of changes with a single anecdote. The trend toward a better life can be seen in most of our own families if we look. For example, I have mild asthma. Recently I slept in a home where there was a dog, and in the middle of the night I woke with a bad cough and shortness of breath. When I realized that it was caused by the dog dander, I took out my twelve dollar pocket inhaler, good for 3,000 puffs, and took one puff. Within ten minutes my lungs were clear. A small miracle. Forty years ago I would have been sleepless and miserable all night, and I would have had to give up the squash-playing that I love so much because exercise causes my worst asthma in the absence of an inhaler . . . Or diabetes. If your child had diabetes a hundred years ago, you had to watch helplessly as the child went blind and died early. Now injections, or even pills, can give the child almost as long and healthy a life as other children . . . Or glasses. Centuries ago you had to give up reading when your eyes got dim as you got to be 40 or 50. Now you can buy magnifying glasses at the drugstore for nine dollars. And you can even wear contact lenses for eye problems and keep your vanity intact. Is there not some condition in your family that in earlier times would have been a lingering misery or a tragedy, that nowadays our increasing knowledge has rendered easily bearable?

With respect to population growth: A dozen competent statistical studies, starting in 1967 with an analysis by Nobel Prize winner Simon Kuznets, agree that there is no negative statistical relationship between economic growth and population growth. There is strong reason to believe that more people have a positive effect in the long run. Population growth does not lower the standard of living—all the evidence agrees. And the evidence supports the view that population growth raises it in the long run.

Incidentally, it was those statistical studies that converted me in about 1968 from working in favor of population control to the point of view that I hold today. I certainly did not come to my current view for any political or religious or ideological reason.

The basic method is to gather data on each country's rate of population growth and its rate of economic growth, and then to examine whether—looking at all the data in the sample together—the countries with high population growth rates have economic growth rates lower than average, and countries with low population growth rates have economic growth rates higher than average. All the studies agree in concluding that this is not so; there is no correlation between economic growth and population growth in the intermediate run.

Of course one can adduce cases of countries that seemingly are exceptions to the pattern. It is the genius of statistical inference, however, to enable us to draw valid generalizations from samples that contain such wide variations in behavior. The exceptions can be useful in alerting us to possible avenues for further analysis, but as long as they are only exceptions, they do not prove that the generalization is not meaningful or useful.

The research-wise person may wonder whether population density is a more meaningful variable than population growth. And indeed, such studies have been done. And again, the statistical evidence directly contradicts the common-sense conventional wisdom. If you make a chart with population density on the horizontal axis and either the income level or the rate of change of income on the vertical axis, you will see that higher density is associated with better rather than poorer economic results.

Check for yourself: Fly over Hong Kong—just a few decades ago a place seemingly without prospects because of insoluble resource problems—and you will marvel at the astounding collection of modern high-rise apartments and office buildings. Take a ride on its excellent smooth-flowing highways for an hour or two, and you will realize that a very dense concentration of human beings does not prevent comfortable existence and exciting economic expansion—as long as the economic system gives individuals the freedom to exercise their talents and to take advantage of opportunities. And the experience of Singapore demonstrates that Hong Kong is not unique. Two such examples do not prove the case, of course. But these dramatic illustrations are backed by the evidence from the aggregate sample of countries, and hence do not mislead us.

(Hong Kong is a special thrill for me because I first saw it in 1955 when I went ashore from a U.S. Navy destroyer. At the time I felt great pity for the thousands who slept every night on the sidewalks or on small boats. It then seemed clear to me, as it must have to almost every observer, that it would be impossible for Hong Kong to surmount its problems—huge masses of impoverished people without jobs, total lack of exploitable natural resources, more refugees pouring across the border each day. But upon returning in 1983, I saw bustling crowds of healthy, vital people full of hope and energy. No cause for pity now.)

The most important benefit of population size and growth is the increase it brings to the stock of useful knowledge. Minds matter economically as much as, or more than, hands or mouths. Progress is limited largely by the availability of trained workers. The more people who enter our population by birth or immigration, the faster will be the rate of progress of our material and cultural civilization.

Here we need a qualification that tends to get overlooked: I do not say that all is well everywhere, and I do not predict that all will be rosy in the future. Children are hungry and sick; people live out lives of physical or intellectual poverty, and lack of opportunity; war or some new pollution may finish us off. What I am saying is that for most relevant economic matters I have checked, the aggregate trends are improving rather than deteriorating.

Also, I don't say that a better future happens automatically or without effort. It will happen because women and men will struggle with problems with muscle and mind, and will probably overcome, as people have over-come in the past—if the social and economic system gives them opportunity to do so.

THE EXPLANATION OF THESE AMAZING TRENDS

Now we need some theory to explain how it can be that economic wel-fare grows along with population, rather than humanity being reduced to misery and poverty as population grows.

The Malthusian theory of increasing scarcity, based on supposedly fixed resources—the theory that the doomsayers rely upon—runs exactly con-trary to the data over the long sweep of history. Therefore it makes sense to prefer another theory.

The theory that fits the facts very well is this: More people, and increased income, cause problems in the short run. Short-run scarcity raises prices. This presents opportunity, and prompts the search for solutions. In a free society, solutions are eventually found. And in the long run the new devel-opments leave us better off than if the problems had not arisen.

To put it differently, in the short run, more consumers mean less of the fixed available stock of goods to be divided among more people. And more workers laboring with the same fixed current stock of capital mean that there will be less output per worker. The latter effect, known as "the law of diminishing returns," is the essence of Malthus's theory as he first set it out.

But if the resources with which people work are not fixed over the period being analyzed, then the Malthusian logic of diminishing returns does not apply. And the plain fact is that, given some time to adjust to shortages, the resource base does not remain fixed. People create more resources of all kinds.

When we take a long-run view, the picture is different and considerably more complex than the simple short-run view of more people implying lower average income. In the very long run, more people almost surely imply more available resources and a higher income for everyone.

I suggest you test this idea against your own knowledge: Do you think that our standard of living would be as high as it is now if the population had never grown from about four million human beings perhaps ten thou-sand years ago? I don't think we'd now have electric light or gas heat or autos or penicillin or travel to the moon or our present life expectancy of over 70 years at birth in rich countries, in comparison to the life expectancy of 20 to 25 years at birth in earlier eras, if population had not grown to its present numbers.

Consider this example of the process by which people wind up with increasing availability rather than decreasing availability of resources.

England was full of alarm in the 1600s at an impending shortage of energy due to the deforestation of the country for firewood. People feared a scarcity of fuel for both heating and for the iron industry. This impending scarcity led to the development of coal.

Then in the mid-1800s the English came to worry about an impending coal crisis. The great English economist, Jevons, calculated that a shortage of coal would bring England's industry to a standstill by 1900; he carefully assessed that oil could never make a decisive difference. Triggered by the impending scarcity of coal (and of whale oil, whose story comes next) ingenious profit-minded people developed oil into a more desirable fuel than coal ever was. And in 1990 we find England exporting both coal and oil.

Another element in the story: Because of increased demand due to population growth and increased income, the price of whale oil for lamps jumped in the 1840s, and the U.S. Civil War pushed it even higher, leading to a whale oil "crisis." This provided incentive for enterprising people to discover and produce substitutes. First came oil from rapeseed, olives, linseed, and camphene oil from pine trees. Then inventors learned how to get coal oil from coal. Other ingenious persons produced kerosene from the rock oil that seeped to the surface, a product so desirable that its price then rose from $.75 a gallon to $2.00. This high price stimulated enterprisers to focus on the supply of oil, and finally Edwin L. Drake brought in his famous well in Titusville, Pennsylvania. Learning how to refine the oil took a while. But in a few years there were hundreds of small refiners in the U.S., and soon the bottom fell out of the whale oil market, the price falling from $2.50 or more at its peak around 1866 to well below a dollar. And in 1993 we see Great Britain exporting both coal and oil.

Here we should note that it was not the English government that developed coal or oil, because governments are not effective developers of new technology. Rather, it was individual entrepreneurs who sensed the need, saw opportunity, used all kinds of available information and ideas, made lots of false starts that were very costly to many of those individuals but not to others, and eventually arrived at coal as a viable fuel—because there were enough independent individuals investigating the matter for at least some of them to arrive at sound ideas and methods. And this happened in the context of a competitive enterprise system that worked to produce what was needed by the public. And the entire process of impending shortage and new solution left us better off than if the shortage problem had never arisen.

THE ROLE OF ECONOMIC FREEDOM

Here we must address another crucial element in the economics of resources and population—the extent to which the political-social-economic system provides personal freedom from government coercion. Skilled persons require an appropriate social and economic framework that provides incentives for working hard and taking risks, enabling their talents to flower and come to fruition. The key elements of such a framework are economic liberty, respect for property, and fair and sensible rules of the market that enforce equally for all.

The world's problem is not too many people, but lack of political and economic freedom. Powerful evidence comes from an extraordinary natural experiment that occurred starting in the 1940s with three pairs of countries that have the same culture and history, and had much the same standard of living when they split apart after World War II—East and West Germany, North and South Korea, Taiwan and China. In each case the centrally planned communist country began with less population "pressure", as measured by density per square kilometer, than did the market-directed economy. And the communist and non-communist countries also started with much the same birth rates.

The market-directed economies have performed much better economically than the centrally planned economies. The economic-political system clearly was the dominant force in the results of the three comparisons. This powerful explanation of economic development cuts the ground from under population growth as a likely explanation of the speed of nations' economic development.

So far we've been discussing the factual evidence. But in 1994 there is an important new element not present twenty years ago. The scientific community of scholars who study population economics now agrees with almost all of what is written above. The statements made above do not represent a single lone voice, but rather the current scientific consensus.

The conclusions offered earlier about agriculture and resources and demographic trends have always represented the consensus of economists in those fields. And now the consensus of population economists also is not far from what is written here.

In 1986, the U.S. National Research Council and the U.S. National Academy of Sciences published a book on population growth and economic development prepared by a prestigious scholarly group. This "official" report reversed almost completely the frightening conclusions of the previous 1971 NAS report. "Population growth at most a minor factor . . ." "The scarcity of exhaustible resources is at most a minor constraint on economic growth," it now says. It found benefits of additional people as well as costs.

A host of review articles by distinguished economic demographers in the past decade have confirmed that this "revisionist" view is indeed consistent with the scientific evidence, though not all the writers would go as far as I do in pointing out the positive long-run effects of population growth. The consensus is more toward a "neutral" judgment. But this is a huge change from the earlier judgment that population growth is economically detrimental.

By 1994, anyone who confidently asserts that population growth damages the economy must turn a blind eye to the scientific evidence.

SUMMARY AND CONCLUSION

In the short run, all resources are limited. An example of such a finite resource is the amount of space allotted to me. The longer run, however, is a different story. The standard of living has risen along with the size of the world's population since the beginning of recorded time. There is no convincing economic reason why these trends toward a better life should not continue indefinitely.

The key theoretical idea is this: The growth of population and of income create actual and expected shortages, and hence lead to price run-ups. A price increase represents an opportunity that attracts profit-minded entrepreneurs to seek new ways to satisfy the shortages. Some fail, at cost to themselves. A few succeed, and the final result is that we end up better off than if the original shortage problems had never arisen. That is, we need our problems though this does not imply that we should purposely create additional problems for ourselves.

I hope that you will now agree that the long-run outlook is for a more abundant material life rather than for increased scarcity, in the United States and in the world as a whole. Of course such progress does not come about automatically. And my message certainly is not one of complacency. In this I agree with the doomsayers—that our world needs the best efforts of all humanity to improve our lot. I part company with them in that they expect us to come to a bad end despite the efforts we make, whereas I expect a continuation of humanity's history of successful efforts. And I believe that their message is self-fulfilling, because if you expect your efforts to fail because of inexorable natural limits, then you are likely to feel resigned; and therefore to literally resign. But if you recognize the possibility—in fact the probability—of success, you can tap large reservoirs of energy and enthusiasm.

Adding more people causes problems, but people are also the means to solve these problems. The main fuel to speed the world's progress is our stock of knowledge, and the brakes are (a) our lack of imagination, and (b) unsound social regulations of these activities. The ultimate resource is people—especially skilled, spirited, and hopeful young people endowed with liberty—who will exert their wills and imaginations for their own benefit, and so inevitably they will benefit not only themselves but the rest of us as well.

REFERENCES

National Research Council, Committee on Population, and Working Group on Population Growth and Economic Development, Population Growth and Economic Development: Policy Questions (Washington, D.C.: National Academy Press, 1986).

Schultz, Theodore W., "The Declining Economic Importance of Land," *Economic Journal,* LXI, December, 1951, pp. 725–740.

Julian L. Simon was a professor at the University of Maryland. His books include *The Ultimate Resource* and *The Economics of Popular Growth.*

Reading 10
FACTS VERSUS FEARS: A REVIEW OF THE GREATEST UNFOUNDED HEALTH SCARES OF RECENT TIMES
Adam J. Lieberman and Simona C. Kwon

This reading was prepared for the American Council on Science and Health.

INTRODUCTION

In a way, this report is a sort of "Greatest Hits" list. But unlike a "Best of . . ." album, put out to celebrate a musician's years-long body of good work, this lineup might be called a "Worst of . . ." Since its founding in 1978, the American Council on Science and Health has been dedicated to separating real, proven health risks such as cigarettes from unfounded health "scares" based on questionable, hypothetical, or even nonexistent scientific evidence. This report summarizes 20 of the most noteworthy scares of the past half century.

In each case we review the charges made against a given product or substance—or even against an entire community. We discuss the basis for the charges, the reactions of the public and the media, and the actual facts as to what risk (if any) ever existed. Where applicable, we give an update on what the latest and most credible scientific studies have to say on each topic. The scares are presented in chronological order, arranged according to the year in which each became a major public issue.

We have chosen these scares because each received great public attention in its day—and each followed its own course to closure in terms of public and regulatory response. (For the same reason we have decided not to discuss certain current scares, such as the furor over breast implants, for which the final chapter has yet to be written.) Some of the scares examined here led to products or substances being banned. In other scares, after an initial panic, consumers shrugged off their fears.

It is interesting to note that these decisions—to ban or to forget—generally depended not on the relative magnitude of the risk but on consumers' understanding of the role that the products in question played in their daily lives. In some cases a very small risk was exaggerated, or the risk was not compared with the benefits to be derived from the substance in question. In other cases the available evidence shows no risk to human health, and the people making the charges knew—or should have known—this all along.

Widespread public fears and concerns over matters of health and safety are not new to our era, of course. But what makes these particular scares unique in comparison with the panics of earlier times is that these specifically involved the products of technology, rather than the natural plagues that claimed so many lives in the past; that they were fueled by modern mass media; and that these scares emerged at a time when Americans enjoyed better health, an ever-increasing life span, a higher standard of living, and a greater scientific understanding of the true causes of human death and disease.

As you read this report, you will see common themes and patterns emerge in the accounts of the scares:

• the indiscriminate extrapolation of laboratory tests involving rodents fed huge doses of a given substance, with the presumption that if a substance caused cancer in those rodents, it also causes cancer in man;

• ignorance of the basic principle of toxicology, "The dose makes the poison," as consumers fretted over the presence of even a single molecule of a substance that might be hazardous in far larger amounts;

• the acceptance, implicit or explicit, of the "precautionary principle," which states: "where there are threats of serious or irreversible environmental damage, lack of full scientific certainty shall not be used as a reason for postponing cost-effective measures to prevent degradation"[1] (bear in mind here that *next to no evidence* can be considered "lack of scientific certainty"); and

• the fear of "synthetic" chemicals, even when some of the same substances exist far more abundantly in nature.

These themes and patterns were all present in the first of our scares, the infamous 1959 "cranberry scare." They continued to pop up in almost every scare of the next three decades, and they reached their zenith with the great Alar scare of 1989.

The response to scares in the post-Alar era has been more muted. This may be due, perhaps, to public "overload" and to growing skepticism in the face of regular front-page health warnings such as the Center for Science in the Public Interest's periodic admonitions against Chinese food, Mexican food, and other popular gustatory diversions.

The purpose of this report is not, of course, merely to reflect on modern society's propensity to fear the unfamiliar. This paper is meant to serve as a cautionary tale of a different kind.

Repeated scares that focus on trivial or nonexistent risks—and the media blitzes and public panics that follow—may actually divert scarce resources away from real, significant public health risks even as they whip up needless anxiety. This report shows just how the American public has been manipulated repeatedly by certain segments of the media, by a handful of scientists outside the scientific mainstream, and by a larger coterie of activists and government regulators, all of whom have frightened the public over hypothetical risks.

This report is intended to make you, the consumer, aware of this continuing pattern. After reading *Facts Versus Fears,* the next time such an alarm flashes across your TV screen, you might just want to mutter, "Been there; done that" and switch the channel.

THE "CRANBERRY SCARE," 1959

Background

Aminotriazole, a weed killer, was first used on cranberry crops in 1957. Because the chemical had not yet been approved for use on crops, growers withheld 30,000 barrels of cranberries found to contain aminotriazole residue. The following year, the chemical was approved. FDA testing showed, however, that when aminotriazole was fed to rats in concentrations of 100 parts per million in the diet, it produced cancer of the thyroid. Although this dose was the equivalent of a human's ingesting 15,000 pounds of berries every day for a number of years, the FDA restricted aminotriazole in cranberry bogs to post-harvest use.[2] No residues were found during 1958.[3]

The Scare

On November 9, 1959, Secretary of Health, Education, and Welfare Arthur Fleming announced that a consignment of berries from Oregon examined by the San Francisco office of the FDA had been found to be contaminated with aminotriazole. Fleming warned that other berries from Oregon and Washington—9 percent of the crop—might also be contaminated. He added that berries from other states—Massachusetts, Wisconsin, and New Jersey—showed no evidence of contamination. But when asked by a reporter whether "a housewife" could be sure of the safety of the cranberries she was buying, Fleming replied, "To be on the safe side, she doesn't buy."

The Reaction

Fleming's comment, which came just 15 days before Thanksgiving, set off a full-fledged panic. State health officials in Ohio and city authorities in San Francisco and Chicago banned cranberry sales. The states of Michigan, Kentucky, and Washington called for voluntary suspensions. Supermarkets and restaurants in New York and other cities pulled products and dishes containing cranberries off their shelves and menus.[4] A nightclub in Chicago even set a one-to-a-customer limit on cranberry cocktails.[5]

Cranberry growers agreed to join the FDA in searching for aminotriazole contamination[6] but were nonetheless furious at Fleming for his comments. The growers demanded an apology, and the Massachusetts Farm Bureau called for Fleming's resignation. Wary of the effect of the scare, other government officials began to backtrack: Secretary of Agriculture Ezra Taft Benson announced that he would have cranberries on his Thanksgiving table.[7] Even the candidates for the 1960 Presidential election got into the act. At campaign stops in Wisconsin, Vice President Richard Nixon ate four helpings of cranberry sauce and Senator John F. Kennedy downed two glasses of cranberry juice.

Cans of cranberry sauce reappeared on supermarket shelves in time for Thanksgiving, complete with labels assuring buyers that the fruit had been inspected and approved. Fleming himself promised to have cranberries on his holiday table.[8] Cranberry growers had initially feared the total loss of the $45 million to $50 million revenue expected from Thanksgiving cranberry sales—60 percent of annual sales[9]—but the actual loss was apparently much less. At least one U.S. senator suggested that the government reimburse growers for any losses,[10] but no such action was taken.

Conclusion

As noted, any risk from aminotriazole was infinitesimal at best, given the enormous amounts of it fed to rats in the tests that resulted in the FDA's declaring it a carcinogen. Additionally, as with many substances that are rodent carcinogens, any hypothetical harm done by aminotriazole is dwarfed by that of far more potent naturally occurring carcinogens. In this case Dr. Edwin Astwood, a professor of medicine at Tufts University, noted that certain turnips naturally contained 100 times as much anti-thyroid potency as did any cranberries contaminated with aminotriazole.[11]

The New York Times (among others) declared early on that Fleming "went too far" in provoking an unnecessary panic. The *Times* noted that even if humans should prove to be as susceptible to the chemical as rats, people would have to consume fantastic quantities of contaminated berries to suffer any ill effects.[12] These attempts to put the matter into perspective were ignored by the wider public, however.

Even in those days, the public suffered from chemo-phobia. One newspaper article noted the influence of "wildlife and conservation groups and . . . pure-food enthusiasts, who believe that chemical residues on agricultural products pose a threat to health."[13] The most important influence, though, was that of the Delaney clause, which had been passed as an amendment to the Federal Food, Drug, and Cosmetic Act the preceding year. It was the Delaney clause that first codified the "mouse as little man" principle: the premise that any substance that causes cancer in rodents at extraordinarily high doses will also cause cancer in humans at more moderate doses. As one report noted, the Delaney clause tied the FDA's hands. The amendment prevented the FDA from "consider[ing] any food safe if it contains even the smallest amount of a substance (specifically, an *additive:* the Delaney Clause was not applied to substances naturally occurring in foods) which tests have shown will produce cancer in test animals."

"Non-contaminated" cranberries soon returned to kitchen tables across America, but a precedent had been set: The public had been taught to fear trace amounts of chemicals regardless of the actual human health risk.

And this boggy little brouhaha laid the groundwork for scares yet to come: It paved the way for many of the other scares discussed in this report.[14]

CYCLAMATES, 1969

Background

Cyclamates (salts of cyclamic acid) are synthetic non-nutritive sweeteners used as a sugar substitute. They were discovered by accident by a researcher in 1937 and approved by the FDA as a drug in 1951. In 1958 they were reclassified as a food additive; at the time, based on their past history of safe use, the FDA declared them to be GRAS (generally recognized as safe) and thus exempt from regulation under the Food, Drug, and Cosmetic Act.[15]

Cyclamates were originally intended only for the use of the obese and diabetics; but as worrying over excess pounds became a national concern in the 1960s, the use of cyclamates grew dramatically. They were used in everything from soft drinks and candy to canned fruits and salad dressings.[16] Between 1963 and 1970, national consumption of cyclamates rose from 5 million to 21 million pounds.[17]

The Scare

In the late 1960s FDA experiments showed that cyclohexamine, a byproduct of cyclamates, caused chromosome damage in male rats,[18] and in June 1969 a study found that some white Swiss mice developed tumors when cyclamate was implanted in their bladders.[19] In both cases, however, the FDA said the route of administration was inappropriate to draw any conclusion—that is, the afflicted rats were exposed in a way that was not comparable to the route of human exposure: ingestion in the diet.

Then, in October 1969, FDA scientist Dr. Jacqueline Verrett appeared on the NBC evening news declaring that baby chicks injected with cyclamate as embryos had suffered gross malformations, displaying the deformed birds to the national television audience.[20] Both FDA Commissioner Dr. Herbert Ley, Jr., and HEW Secretary Robert Finch criticized Dr. Verrett for going to the media before subjecting her findings to peer-reviewed scrutiny, and both men defended the safety of cyclamate.

A few days later Abbott Laboratories, the manufacturer of cyclamate, released a study showing that 8 out of 240 rats fed a mixture of ten parts cyclamate to one part saccharin (the mixture most often used in food products) developed bladder tumors. As with all tests of this type, the rats were ingesting a dosage far higher than that of equivalent human consumption; in this case, it was the equivalent of 50 cans of diet soda per day.

On October 18, 1969, Finch declared that under the Delaney clause he was obliged to remove cyclamate from the market.[21] The following year the sale of cyclamate as a prescription product to dieters and diabetics was also banned.[22]

The Reaction

Except for the manufacturers of cyclamate-containing products, one of whom was stuck with $31.5 million worth of unusable canned fruits, the public reaction to the cyclamate ban was generally positive. Even though, at the time, nearly 75 percent of Americans used cyclamate in one product or another,[23] nearly 80 percent of the public felt "gratitude for the government protection." At a time when the "back-to-nature" movement in general was picking up steam, the ban dovetailed nicely with the idea that anything "artificial" was dangerous. Many scientific publications, however, were critical of the FDA for acting so precipitously.[24]

And studies of cyclamates continued. Subsequent, large-scale tests on rodents failed to duplicate the results of the 1969 studies; none of the new studies showed any tumors that could be linked to cyclamates.[25] As a result, numerous scientific bodies—among them the National Cancer Institute,[26] the United Nations Food and Agriculture Organization, the World Health Organization, the FDA's Center for Food Safety and Applied Nutrition, and the National Research Council of the National Academy of Sciences—have all declared that that evidence shows cyclamates not to be carcinogenic.

As a result of these studies, Abbott Laboratories has on several occasions petitioned the FDA to revoke the ban on cyclamates; each time, the petition has been rejected. However, in Canada and in the nations of the European Community (EC), cyclamates are once again available; the EC, FAO, and WHO have set an acceptable daily intake of 11 milligrams per kilogram of body weight per day.

Conclusion

Experiments must be subject to peer review and be reproducible to be considered valid. In the case of the studies indicting cyclamates, neither criterion was met. All subsequent studies have drawn conclusions contrary to those that suggested that cyclamates were carcinogens.

The loss of cyclamates did not cause much of an uproar, both because of the mood of the times and because most consumers quickly adjusted by switching to saccharin—which did not become the subject of its own scare until 1977 (see section on saccharin).

SACCHARIN, 1977

Background

Saccharin is a non-caloric, white crystalline powder 300 times sweeter than sugar. It was the first artificial sweetener marketed in the U.S. and was declared "generally recognized as safe" (GRAS) in 1958.[27] As with cyclamates, its use by the general public increased rapidly during the 1960s, although its popularity was not as great as that of cyclamates due to its bitter and metallic aftertaste.[28] After the cyclamates ban, the use of saccharin as a sugar substitute increased dramatically.

The Scare

Almost immediately after the cyclamate scare (see earlier article), saccharin became the next target. A 1970 study suggested that saccharin caused bladder cancer in mice. When a 1972 study showed that it also caused bladder cancer in rats, the FDA removed it from the GRAS list. Then, after a 1977 Canadian study showed similar results, the FDA moved to ban saccharin altogether, basing the decision on the Delaney clause prohibition on the use of food additives that cause cancer in animals. Again, the amounts ingested by the rodents were enormous, up to 5 percent of their total diets.[29]

The Reaction

Unlike the generally agreeable response to the cyclamate ban, the public reaction to the FDA's proposed action on saccharin was overwhelmingly negative. Consumers voted first with their wallets, "sweeping the shelves clean," as one housewife recalls, of pink saccharin packets and any saccharin-containing products in an attempt to stock up against the coming ban.[30] Diabetics lobbied Congress to reverse the ban, given that no other nonsugar sweetener was available. And the diabetics were joined by many weight-conscious members of the general public: During 1977 Congress received more mail on the saccharin issue than on any other topic.[31]

Under public pressure, Congress imposed a moratorium on the ban, instead requiring that saccharin-containing products carry a warning label. Meanwhile, continued studies of saccharin show that while it clearly is a carcinogen in male rats (although a very weak one, in terms of the dose required to produce tumors), it has not been shown to produce tumors in female rats or in any other species. Many scientists believe that these tumors are due to two proteins found in the urine of male rats, but not found in humans or other animals, that react with high levels of saccharin to produce crystals that damage the bladder.[32]

Furthermore, human epidemiological studies have failed to show a link between bladder cancer and heavy saccharin use. For example, people born in Denmark during World War II (when sugar was largely unavailable) and diabetics, who have been constant users of this sweetener for several decades, have failed to show higher-than-normal rates of bladder cancer. In another study, 3,000 individuals recently diagnosed with bladder cancer were found not to show heavier use of saccharin than members of a control group without bladder cancer.[33]

As a result of these findings, the FDA withdrew its proposal to ban saccharin, although the Congressionally imposed warning label remains in place.[34] Saccharin continues to be available, although its use in the U.S. has decreased since 1983, when the FDA approved aspartame, a sugar substitute with no aftertaste.

Conclusion

The charges against saccharin and the research used to justify its banning illustrate the many problems policy makers have when they indiscriminately extrapolate results from animals to man. These include:

- the enormous doses necessary for such experiments—doses so large that they may overwhelm the animal's natural defenses—and;
- the question of whether a substance that is a carcinogen in one species is necessarily a carcinogen in others, given the physiological differences between species, and especially between rodents and humans.

There is also a regulatory "double standard" implicit in the fact that many "natural" substances—everyday items such as table pepper and vitamins A and D among them—have also been proved to be rodent carcinogens under such testing regimens; but these natural substances are not subject to the sort of regulatory action that would be taken with a synthetic additive.

What was different in the saccharin case was that the public viewed saccharin, unlike most "artificial" chemicals, as a product it needed and wanted. Saccharin served a purpose in people's lives, and they strenuously objected to the efforts being made to remove it from the market. This contrasts with other banned substances that were implicated as carcinogens on equally dubious evidence but that elicited less public understanding regarding their purpose or use. Today's highly urbanized public has little understanding of the food production system, for example, or of the vital role pesticides and other agricultural chemicals play in that system. The public is thus willing to fear the worst when such a substance is implicated as a carcinogen.

HAIR DYES, 1977

Background

Commercial hair dyes have been available since about 1920. The key ingredients in most permanent dyes—colors that last, until the hair grows out—are so-called "coal-tar" dyes (actually petroleum derivatives). Under the Food, Drug, and Cosmetic Act of 1938, which first placed cosmetic products under federal regulation, products containing coal-tar dyes must carry a warning label noting that they may cause skin irritation in some individuals.[35] Today, anywhere from 20 to 60 percent of Americans are estimated to use some type of hair coloring; most of it contains coal-tar dyes.[36]

The Scare

In 1975 students in a biochemistry class at the University of California at Berkeley engaged in a class project in which common household products were tested on bacteria to see if they caused genetic mutations. A permanent hair dye was the only substance, other than cigarette tar, to cause such a mutagenic reaction. Subsequent tests showed similar mutagenic reactions in bacteria from many such dyes.

The National Cancer Institute began testing 13 coal-tar chemicals on laboratory rodents. In late 1977 they published a study reporting that seven of the 13 caused tumors in the animals. The most potent of the tested chemicals was 4-methoxy-m-phenylenediamine-sulfate (4-MMPD), which caused thyroid and skin tumors in 24 percent of the rodents.[37] The FDA announced in early 1978 that all dyes containing 4-MMPD would carry a warning label noting that it was an animal carcinogen. Before the label order could go into effect, however, hair-dye manufacturers responded by reformulating their products, removing 4-MMPD as well as three other chemicals commonly used in the dyes and implicated in the rodent tests.

The Reaction

This was not enough for some consumer activists, who accused hair-care companies of using substitute chemicals that were as hazardous as the substances removed. Dr. Benjamin Van Durren of New York University's Institute of Environmental Medicine claimed there was "not one iota" of difference between the replacement chemicals and those they replaced, even though the replacement chemicals tested negative as animal carcinogens.

The cosmetics companies objected to the methodology of the original tests, noting that the rodents *drank* the dye—obviously not the method of human exposure. Although hair-dye chemicals applied to the scalp can penetrate the skin, an earlier FDA test had shown that only 3 percent of the dye was absorbed, and about half of this was excreted in urine. Furthermore, the doses used on the laboratory rodents were the equivalent of a woman's drinking 25 bottles of hair dye every day for her entire life.

At the same time, epidemiological studies were launched to assess whether regular users of dyes were suffering a greater incidence of cancer. Two early studies from Great Britain and Canada failed to show that women using hair dye faced a greater risk of cancer; a third study indicated that women over 50 years old who had used dyes for 10 years or more had a greater incidence of breast cancer. All three studies were limited by the small number of subjects involved. The public concern over the issue subsequently died down, although henna and other "natural" plant-based colorings, which are not as long-lasting, gradually became more popular.

Conclusion

Epidemiological studies continued in an attempt to assess whether the dyes— old or reformulated—ever posed a cancer risk. In a 1992 study of 373 women with non-Hodgkin's lymphoma, researchers concluded that women who used hair dyes had a 50 percent greater chance of developing the disease,[38] but the FDA said that that study "does not allow the establishment of a causal link between hair dye and increased cancer"[39] and so refused to impose a warning label on hair-care products. A much larger study carried out by the FDA and the American Cancer Society showed that "women who use hair dyes do not have an overall greater risk of dying from cancer," although a much smaller subgroup—those who used black hair dyes for more than 20 years—showed an increase in non-Hodgkin's lymphoma and multiple myeloma.

Most recently, Brigham and Women's Hospital conducted a study involving more than 99,000 women and specifically designed to determine whether a link existed between cancer and hair dyes. That study showed no greater risk of blood or lymph cancers among users of dyes.[40] The National Cancer Institute is currently on record as concluding that, while further research is needed in this area, "no recommendation to change hair dye use can be made at this time."

LOVE CANAL, 1978

Background

Love Canal took its name from William Love, an entrepreneur who in the 1890s had an unsuccessful plan to build a massive city near Niagara Falls. The unfinished canal that was dug in the area in Love's time was used between 1942 and 1953 by both the Hooker Chemical Company and the U.S. military to dispose of industrial and chemical wastes, which were sealed under clay lining.

In 1957, as the population of the surrounding area grew, Hooker sold the property above the canal for $1 to the local school board to build a school on the site with the caveat that the land should not be excavated due to the wastes buried underneath. Despite Hooker's warning, the city of Niagara Falls subsequently constructed sanitary and storm sewers at the site, disturbing the wastes.[41]

The Scare

Starting in 1976, local residents began to complain of chemical odors from the landfill, and of chemicals seeping into basements. A local reporter began to write about suspected cases of illness among residents of the canal area. In response to these reports, in 1978 the New York State Health Commissioner called for the evacuation of families, pregnant women, and young children from the area immediately surrounding the canal. Later that year the state announced the relocation of all families living within a two-block radius of the canal.

These announcements led to a ripple effect throughout the community, with homes outside the immediate area losing value. Residents conducted their own informal surveys, which appeared to show elevated incidence of numerous ailments.[42] A report by Dr. Beverly Paigan in 1979 found a high rate of birth defects and miscarriages among Love Canal residents. The study was not a scientific, controlled study, however; it was based only on anecdotal reports from interviews with families in the area.[43] In May 1980 an EPA study reported possible chromosome damage among Love Canal residents; two days later another EPA study concluded that a degree of peripheral nerve damage existed among residents.

Reaction

The two EPA stories immediately became national news; in Love Canal itself, hysteria ensued, with two EPA officials being "involuntarily detained" for several hours. A few days later, the EPA announced that 2,500 residents would be temporarily relocated, at a cost of $3 to $5 million. (The relocation eventually became permanent, at a cost of over $30 million.)[44]

Was there a public health justification for these actions? Both of the EPA studies have since been criticized by other health and scientific authorities, not only for being released prior to peer review, but for errors in statistical analysis, for small sample size, and for improperly drawing conclusions that were in some cases contrary to the evidence. (The chromosome study, for example, actually found that cases of chromosome damage were *lower* overall among Love Canal residents than among a control group.) Subsequent, peer-reviewed studies from the New York State Department of Health failed to show any abnormal health trends among Love Canal residents. And additional studies made in later years by the Centers for Disease Control, the American Medical Association, and the National Research Council reached the same conclusion.[45]

Conclusion

In 1982 the EPA conducted a study showing that outside the area immediately surrounding the canal, there was no unusually high level of chemical contamination. By 1990, after many court battles with environmental groups, a New York state agency created to manage homes near the canal began putting houses on the market.

Despite the obstacle of negative publicity and of banks refusing to grant mortgages for fear of being held liable for environmental contamination,[46] by June 1994, 193 out of 280 available homes had been sold. Appraisers originally deducted 20 percent from house prices because of the location, but this later was reduced to 15 percent as demand increased. Some 30 percent of the purchasers were pre-1980 residents.[47]

The legal battles that have gone on since 1980 also appear to be winding down. In March 1994 a federal judge rejected a claim of $250 million in punitive damages filed by New York state against Occidental Chemical, which had purchased Hooker in 1968.[48] Occidental settled out of court with the EPA in December 1995, agreeing to pay $129 million to cover the costs of cleaning up the site in exchange for the federal and state governments dropping all other claims against the company.[49]

One immediate result of the 1980 panic—a result that remains not only a continuing legacy but a burden—is the so-called "Superfund." Authorized by Congress just months after Love Canal hit the headlines, Superfund spends about $1.7 billion annually—about what the National Cancer Institute spends on research and development—to clean up approximately 2,000 waste sites. Today, over 15 years later, most of the sites have not been reclaimed; and most of the budget has been spent on legal and consulting fees. It remains unclear whether there will be any benefit to public health if and when all the sites are ever cleaned up.[50]

Efforts have been made to reform the Superfund program, but so long as any attempt at reform is portrayed as a means of getting polluters "off the hook"—as EPA head Carol Browner recently charged—rather than as an attempt to put the public health risks from such sites into perspective, any such change seems unlikely.

ALAR, 1989

Background

Alar was the trade name for daminozide, a growth regulator of ripening apples first developed in the 1960s. It was used to prevent apples from dropping off the tree prematurely and rotting prior to harvest. Alar went through two years of FDA carcinogenicity tests and was approved as safe by the FDA in 1968.

In 1973 a study showed that UMDH, a byproduct of Alar, caused blood vessel, lung, and kidney tumors in mice. Subsequent EPA analysis of this study declared it to be flawed, however, because the mice had been treated with such a high dosage of UMDH that the "maximum tolerated dose" (MTD) was exceeded by eight-fold and the toxicity of the high dose might have caused the tumors.[51] (For any substance, no matter how benign, a maximum tolerated dose exists above which the substance will damage tissues merely from its high concentration.[52] Current guidelines for conducting bioassays for carcinogenic effects specify that the maximum tested dose should not exceed the MTD.)

Further tests conducted by the National Cancer Institute in 1978 and by the EPA in 1986 also failed to indicate that Alar was a carcinogen.[53] Nevertheless, the EPA insisted on further tests—tests in which mice were given doses of UMDH at four to eight times the MTD, or 133,000 to 266,000 times the highest estimated daily intake of UMDH by preschool children.[54] To put it another way, a child would have to drink 19,000 quarts of apple juice a day for life to equal this degree of exposure.

At four times the MTD one mouse out of a group of 45 developed a benign lung tumor. At eight times the MTD—close to the level of the discredited 1973 study—11 out of 52 mice developed either benign or malignant tumors. Unfortunately for the other mice in the experiment, 80 percent of the mice died from toxicity, not cancer.

The EPA acknowledged that the study may have been compromised by such high doses but concluded nonetheless that Alar posed a risk of 45 cancers per one million exposed humans. The agency ordered Alar's manufacturer, Uniroyal, to phase out its use by July 31, 1990.

The Scare

This gradual phase-out didn't satisfy the Natural Resources Defense Council, however. The NRDC had been calling for years for an EPA ban on Alar. Then, on February 26, 1989, over 50 million Americans saw a segment on CBS's *60 Minutes* called "A is for Apple." The program labeled Alar "the most potent cancer-causing agent in our food supply" and called it a cause of childhood cancer. The source for these allegations was the NRDC report *Intolerable Risk: Pesticides in Our Children's Food*, which the NRDC had pre-released exclusively to CBS with the assistance of Fenton Communications, a public-relations firm hired to help coordinate the effort.

The Reaction

Fenton and the NRDC achieved their goal to have "the [Alar] 'story' have a life of its own" far beyond their wildest dreams. In the days following the *60 Minutes* broadcast the claims in the NRDC report were repeated by virtually every major print and broadcast outlet. Fenton also enlisted some high-profile help: actress Meryl Streep and the wife of NBC newsman Tom Brokaw, who formed a group called Mothers and Others For Pesticide Limits.

Public reaction verged on the hysterical. One consumer called the International Apple Institute to ask if it was safe to discard apple juice in the kitchen sink, or whether it was necessary to take it to a toxic waste dump.

A parent sent state troopers chasing after her child's school bus to confiscate the forbidden fruit her child was carrying. Fenton and NRDC even received an added bonus when the FDA announced that some grapes from Chile were tainted. Although the Chilean fruit had nothing to do with Alar, the incident fed the general atmosphere of panic.[55]

Not everyone joined in the chorus of alarmism, however. Many science reporters questioned the methodology of the studies on which the EPA and NRDC had based their conclusions. Even other environmentalist groups (such as the Environmental Defense Fund) declared that the NRDC's data were inconclusive. And a few days after the 60 Minutes report, the National Research Defense Council declared that there was "no evidence that pesticides or natural toxins in food contribute significantly to cancer risk in the United States."[56]

In an unusual step, 60 Minutes devoted a second broadcast to the issue. Several critics of the earlier program, including ACSH president Dr. Elizabeth Whelan, appeared on the second show. But 60 Minute's correspondent Ed Bradley spent much of the program impugning the motives of the critics, suggesting that they were being influenced by the chemical industry.

Finally, under pressure from apple growers—who were suffering losses whether or not they used Alar—Uniroyal withdrew Alar from use on edible products in June of 1989.[57] When the dust had cleared, apple growers had lost an estimated $250 million. Apple processors had lost another $125 million. Some growers who had owned their farms for generations lost them to foreclosure. And the U.S. taxpayer lost, too: The U.S. Department of Agriculture made an emergency purchase of $15 million worth of leftover apples.[58]

This was the end of Alar—but it was not the end of the story. Since 1989 a stream of criticism by independent scientists and scientific authorities has continued to be leveled at the NRDC and the EPA. In Great Britain a group appointed by Parliament declined to ban Alar, stating that, unlike the EPA, " we don't always make the assumption that animal data are transferable to man" or that high-dose responses can predict low-dose responses.[59] A United Nations panel of scientists from the World Health Organization and the Food and Agriculture Organization also concluded that Alar was not oncogenic (tumor-causing) in mice.

In subsequent years, the anti-Alar campaign has been criticized on the editorial page of Science magazine (which compared the NRDC's actions to those of an embezzler); by former Surgeon General C. Everett Koop, the chairman of the National Safe Kids Campaign; and by the senior medical advisor to the American Medical Association.[60] In a 1993 article in ECO magazine, New York Times reporter Keith Schneider, a veteran of the environmental movement, described the NRDC report on Alar as "specious" and as having "not much scientific evidence."[61]

Even the EPA, although bound by the Delaney clause definition of a carcinogen and so unable to change its judgment on Alar, nonetheless released a new toxicological analysis in late 1991 that showed Alar to be only half as potent as earlier estimates had indicated.[62]

The NRDC continued to defend its action, noting that the Supreme Court had recently refused to hear an appeal of a defamation suit filed by Washington state apple growers against CBS, the NRDC, and Fenton.[63] However, the court's denial had been based on the conclusion that as long as the EPA held Alar to be a carcinogen, the CBS report could not be proved false.

Alar itself is clearly too stigmatized ever to be returned to the market, but there is no doubt that public perception has changed since 1989. The climate has changed to the point where a writer in the *Columbia Journalism Review* recently bemoaned the continued attention given to exposing the NRDC's false claims about Alar. The *CJR* piece alleged that this was due to a "concerted dis-information campaign by industry trade groups,"[64] but did so without providing a single example either of how the criticisms of the anti-Alar campaign were in error or of how "industry" groups were responsible for pointing out the campaign's scientific inaccuracies.

The *Columbia Journalism Review* article was correct though, in pointing out that the media have become far more circumspect about giving uncritical publicity to health scares without first consulting with mainstream scientists. In one recent example, the alarmist *Our Stolen Future*—a book alleging that chlorinated compounds in the environment posed grave health risks to humans—was released in the spring of 1996. The book's release was handled with public-relations assistance from Fenton Communications. Most of the media reports on *Our Stolen Future* included the views of scientists skeptical of the book's claims and made note of Fenton Communications' activities during the Alar scare.[65]

Conclusion

Back on the apple farm the effects of Alar's loss are still being felt. Farmers from Ohio to New Hampshire are reporting decimation of their crops and, ironically, a need to use additional pesticides to enable the trees to hold their fruit.[66] And Alar lives on as a symbol: a symbol, first, of a model of risk assessment increasingly under criticism from scientists as having no relation to actual human cancer risks and, second, of the manipulation of the media by interest groups acting in contravention of the consensus of mainstream science.

The fallout from the Alar campaign was also a blow to the entire "mouse-as-a-little-man" premise. As the public followed the Alar story, it learned of the basis for the government's risk estimates, and it began to see how poorly such tests actually predicted human cancer risks. More generally, many consumers started to grow skeptical of the countless health scares popping up almost daily in the media.

ASBESTOS IN SCHOOLS, 1993

Background

From 1940 to 1973 schools across the United States were required to have asbestos insulation as a fire safety measure.[67] Asbestos was also widely used in many schools in tiles and plaster.[68] The EPA banned the use of asbestos in schools in 1973; by the late 1970s the agency started formulating regulations in an attempt to reduce the exposure of schoolchildren to the substance.[69]

In 1982 the EPA required that all schools be inspected for friable (easily crumbled) asbestos. In 1984 Congress passed the Asbestos School Hazard Abatement Act to provide financial assistance to schools with serious asbestos hazards. And in 1986 Congress passed the Asbestos Hazard Emergency Response Act (AHERA), which required all private and public schools to inspect for asbestos, develop asbestos management plans, and implement appropriate actions. By 1990 it was estimated that the cost of such abatement work was over $6 billion.[70]

The public health benefit of all this was unclear, as asbestos experts have estimated that the lifetime risk to schoolchildren exposed to 0.001 fibers of chrysotile asbestos per milliliter of air for a minimum of 10 years is one additional death in 100,000 (that's three times less than the risk of being struck by lightning); and, in fact, most schools had asbestos levels far less than 0.001 fibers per milliliter.

The Scare

An EPA report showed that post-removal levels of asbestos were often significantly higher than pre-removal levels; thus, poorly conducted asbestos removals may actually increase health risks by releasing more particles into the air.[71] Additionally, while EPA guidelines do not require removal of asbestos if the materials are not significantly damaged, many school districts misunderstood the guidelines, taking them as a mandate to remove all asbestos. This misunderstanding led to unnecessary expense and to the diversion of school funds from other needs.[72]

In August 1993 it was revealed that an independent contractor to whom the New York City Board of Education had paid $2 million to inspect the city schools for asbestos had failed to perform the inspection properly. (The contractor did, of course, pocket the city's money.) To avoid being held in contempt of the 1986 AHERA law, New York's Mayor Dinkins announced that no school would be allowed to open in September until it had been inspected and found safe by both the Department of Environmental Protection and the Health Department. As a result, the opening of school for nearly 1 million New York City schoolchildren was delayed by two weeks, with a few schools remaining shuttered even longer, their students placed in other buildings.[73]

The Reaction

Most schoolchildren were probably grateful for the respite; most scientists were less so. The American Medical Association had already declared that the type of low-level exposure found in school buildings, averaging 0.0005 fibers per milliliter (probably no more than the level in ambient air in Manhattan), did not pose a health hazard. This was especially true because the type of asbestos used in schools—chrysotile, or "white" asbestos—is considered far less hazardous than other types of asbestos—specifically, crocidolite and amosite. (Chrysotile makes up 95 percent of the asbestos ever used in the U.S.; it is easily expelled by the lungs rather than attaching itself to lung tissue.)[74]

Conclusion

The 1993 New York City asbestos scare may have done some good in the sense that it alerted many in the general community to the hazards of hyperbolizing about environmental risks. Many parents asked whether such a hypothetical risk was worth disrupting their and their children's lives for. The asbestos abatement laws (and the $4-to-6-billion-dollar-a-year abatement industry) remain in place; but more people are aware now that asbestos, as chemist P.J. Wingate puts it, is "like a big sleeping dog. If not stirred up, it does no harm. If hammered or sawed on, it may bite anyone near it."[75]

CELLULAR PHONES, 1993

Background

Since a 1979 report suggested that electromagnetic fields (EMFs) from power lines might increase the risk of childhood cancer,[76] sporadic scares have developed over the health effects of a wide variety of electrical appliances—devices ranging from electric blankets to computer terminals and from electric razors to alarm clocks.

Subsequent studies have shown methodological errors in the 1979 report: It failed to account for other carcinogenic factors, and studies of occupational exposure among electrical workers and others exposed to high levels of EMFs have given conflicting data.[77] Scientists have also pointed out that such electromagnetic fields are far too weak to affect human tissue by any of the known mechanisms by which the far stronger X-rays and ultraviolet radiation can break apart cellular components and cause cancer.[78] But the most publicized health scare involving an electromagnetic field was based on no scientific data at all.

The Scare

David Reynard of Tampa, Florida, gave his wife a cellular phone when she became pregnant in 1988. Two years later she was diagnosed with a brain tumor. The tumor was located just behind her right ear, where she typically had placed the phone's antenna.[79] After his wife's death, Reynard filed suit against the phone's manufacturer, alleging that electromagnetic energy from the phone's antenna had caused the cancer. On January 21, 1993, Reynard appeared on CNN's *Larry King Live* to air his claims; in the weeks that followed, three similar lawsuits were filed by cellular phone users who had developed brain tumors in similar locations.[80]

The Reaction

These anecdotal charges were, as one report noted, "not the kind of evidence that would be accepted by the *New England Journal of Medicine*"; but, for a time, it didn't matter. The authoritative voice of Larry King intoning, "cellular phones can kill you" struck a nerve.

One national journalist who had "become addicted to her cellular phone" described it as "yet another technology that is out to get us."[81] Sales of the phones, which had been growing at a rate of from 20 to 70 percent a year since 1982, fell off sharply. Stock prices of the three largest cellular companies dropped about 10 percent during the week following the King broadcast.[82] Even more than Alar, the scare quickly entered the national consciousness, perhaps because of the image of the cellular phone as a "yuppie accessory." One entrepreneur offered a device to shield users' heads from the supposedly deadly antennae.[83]

Congressional hearings were held. The FDA, the National Cancer Institute, and the EPA all declared that there was no reason to put your phone on hold,[84] although an FDA spokesperson did suggest that if consumers were concerned, "they should pay attention to their usage."[85] It was also noted that while the number of brain cancers had increased slightly between 1973 and 1989—from five per 100,000 to six per 100,000—there had been no change in the pattern of location of the tumors—as might be expected if the phones were, indeed, the culprit.[86]

At present it is not possible to tell whether an individual's cancer arose because of cellular phone use, or whether it would have happened anyway. At the current brain cancer incidence rate, about 180 cases would be expected among the approximately 3 million owners of hand-held cellular phones—whether or not they actually used their phones.[87]

Conclusion

Cellular trade associations promised to spend $25 million for research into cellular safety. An independent research entity was organized to implement a research program, including laboratory and epidemiology studies.[88]

Within months, however, the scare was largely forgotten. By mid-1993 sales of cellular phones were up 30 percent over the previous year, stock prices had recovered, and consumers had apparently lost concern. When one phone company offered its customers a free phone if they signed up for cellular service and offered a choice of three models, most customers chose the pocket model—with the antenna next to the user's head—over two other models with different configurations.[89]

Very few studies on electromagnetic fields are relevant to the evaluation of exposure to radio frequency (the frequency used by cellular phones) and the development of cancer in humans. Cancer studies in animals provide no clear evidence of an increase in tumor incidence.[90]

But while no study has proved that the electromagnetic fields from phones or other devices are harmful, it remains impossible to prove a negative, such as that EMFs are *not* harmful. And frustrating the efforts to evaluate the effects of EMFs are difficulties in the design, implementation, and interpretation of epidemiological studies—particularly with respect to identifying populations with substantial exposures.[91]

The brief life of the cellular phone scare may be a sign that consumers are beginning to show a more measured reaction to reports of this type. At the present time there is no convincing evidence that EMFs from cellular phones are harmful.[92] Indeed, as suggested by a recent study reported in the *New England Journal of Medicine,* if there is any significant danger from cellular phones, it is from trying to drive while talking on one: The study showed that drivers who use cellular phones have four times the risk of accidents as drivers who do not.[93]

The American Council on Science and Health is a consumer education consortium. Its top priority is to help Americans distinguish between real and hypothetical health risks.

Reading 11
DDT BAN IS GENOCIDAL
Steven Milloy

As First-World children eagerly anticipate the holiday season, millions of Third-World children are about to be condemned to certain death from malaria by international environmental elitists.

The World Wildlife Fund (WWF), Greenpeace, Physicians for Social Responsibility, and 250 other environmental groups will advocate the insecticide DDT be banned at next week's United Nations Environment Program meeting in Johannesburg. The meeting's aim is a treaty banning or restricting so-called persistent organic chemicals.

Malaria control experts oppose a DDT ban, arguing that spraying DDT in houses is inexpensive and highly effective in controlling malaria—especially in sub-Saharan Africa where 1 in 20 children die from malaria. Unfortunately, the eco-elites have out-maneuvered and outgunned public health advocates. Saving lives doesn't interest DDT opponents, who insist on recycling junk science to achieve their ill-considered goal of a pesticide-free world.

"DDT is a persistent, bioaccumulative, hormone-disrupting chemical," alleges the director of the WWF's anti-DDT effort. "It is associated in the public's mind with weakened eggshells and declining bird populations . . ." he added.

But there never was, and still isn't, a scientific basis for DDT fear-mongering.

The "public's mind" was first polluted with misinformation about DDT by Rachel Carson in her 1962 book, *Silent Spring*. Carson incorrectly alleged that DDT harmed bird reproduction and caused cancer. Carson wrote: "Dr. [James] DeWitt's now classic experiments [show] that exposure to DDT, even when doing no observable harm to the birds, may seriously affect reproduction. Quail, into whose diet DDT was introduced throughout the breeding season, survived and even produced normal numbers of fertile eggs. But few of the eggs hatched."

DeWitt actually reported no significant difference in egg hatching between birds fed DDT and birds not fed DDT.

Carson predicted a cancer epidemic that could hit "practically 100 percent" of the human population. This prediction hasn't materialized, no doubt because it was based on a 1961 epidemic of liver cancer in middle-aged rainbow trout—later attributed to aflatoxin. There is no credible evidence that DDT poses a cancer risk whatsoever.

As wrong as Carson was, the Environmental Protection Agency's action against DDT—the precedent for next week's meeting to ban the chemical—was worse. Anti-DDT activism led to hearings before an EPA administrative law judge in 1971–72. After 7 months and 9,000 pages of testimony, the judge concluded "DDT is not a carcinogenic hazard to man . . . DDT is not a mutagenic or teratogenic hazard to man . . . The use of DDT under the regulations involved here do not have a deleterious effect on freshwater fish, estuarine organisms, wild birds, or other wildlife."

Despite the exculpatory ruling, then-EPA administrator William Ruckelshaus banned DDT. Ruckelshaus didn't attend the hearings or read the transcript. He refused to release the memos used to make his decision, even rebuffing a Department of Agriculture request through the Freedom of Information Act. As it turns out, Ruckelshaus belonged to the Environmental Defense Fund (EDF). Ruckelshaus solicited donations for the anti-pesticide activist group on personal stationery stating, "EDF's scientists blew the whistle on DDT by showing it to be a cancer hazard, and three years later, when the dust had cleared, EDF had won." The WWF now alleges DDT disrupts hormonal processes to wreak havoc on immune, reproductive and nervous systems in laboratory animals, citing a 1999 report by the National Research Council.

The allegation conveniently overlooks the report's main conclusion that the scientific evidence is inadequate to suggest that low doses of chemicals typically found in the environment pose any risk. It's not surprising, after all, that animals administered high doses of chemicals develop all sorts of ill effects; they've essentially been poisoned.

The WWF's chicanery doesn't end with the science. Publicly, the WWF claims it backed off the demand of a DDT ban by 2007 in favor of regulatory controls. Don't be fooled.

The would-be controls are so onerous and costly for the Third World that they would operate as a de facto ban. Of the 23 countries using DDT, only nine countries so far asked for exemptions under the impending treaty. The others either have stockpiled DDT in advance or have been scared off by the burdensome regulatory scheme, according to Roger Bate of FightingMalaria.org.

Donor agencies such as the U.S. Agency for International Development (AID) have pressured Belize, Bolivia, and Mozambique not to use DDT— or risk losing their aid money, adds Bate.

The AID's blackmail is eerily similar to its 1970s view that the failure of the Global Malaria Eradication Program (1956–1969) was a blessing in disguise. "Better off dead than riotously reproducing," an AID official said.

A committee of the National Academy of Sciences wrote in 1970, "To only a few chemicals does man owe as great a debt as to DDT . . . in a little more than two decades, DDT has prevented 500 million deaths due to malaria that otherwise would have been inevitable."

The WWF et al. often exploit "the children" as a stalking horse for their dubious agenda. Their effort to ban DDT is a chilling reminder of this cynicism.

Steven Milloy is a biostatistician, lawyer, and publisher of Junkscience.com.

Reading 12
CARS AND THEIR ENEMIES
James Q. Wilson

Imagine the country we now inhabit—big, urban, prosperous—with one exception: the automobile has not been invented. We have trains and bicycles, and some kind of self-powered buses and trucks, but no private cars driven by their owners for business or pleasure. Of late, let us suppose, someone has come forward with the idea of creating the personal automobile. Consider how we would react to such news.

Libertarians might support the idea, but hardly anyone else. Engineers would point out that such cars, if produced in any significant number, would zip along roads just a few feet—perhaps even a few inches—from one another; the chance of accidents would not simply be high, it would be certain. Public-health specialists would estimate that many of these accidents would lead to serious injuries and deaths. No one could say in advance how common they would be, but the best experts might guess that the number of people killed by cars would easily exceed the number killed by murderers. Psychologists would point out that if any young person were allowed to operate a car, the death rate would be even higher, as youngsters—those between the ages of sixteen and twenty-four—are much more likely than older persons to be impulsive risk-takers who find pleasure in reckless bravado. Educators would explain that, though they might try by training to reduce this youthful death rate, they could not be optimistic they would succeed.

Environmentalists would react in horror to the idea of automobiles powered by the internal combustion engine, apparently the most inexpensive method. Such devices, because they burn fuel incompletely, would eject large amounts of unpleasant gases into the air, such as carbon monoxide, nitrogen oxide, and sulfur dioxide. Other organic compounds, as well as clouds of particles, would also enter the atmosphere to produce unknown but probably harmful effects. Joining in this objection would be people who would not want their view spoiled by the creation of a network of roads.

Big-city mayors would add their own objections, though these would reflect their self-interest as much as their wisdom. If people could drive anywhere from anywhere, they would be able to live wherever they wished. This would produce a vast exodus from the large cities, led in all likelihood by the most prosperous, and thus the most tax-productive, citizens. Behind would remain people who, being poorer, were less mobile. Money would depart, but problems would remain.

Governors, pressed to keep taxes down and still fund costly health, welfare, educational, and criminal-justice programs, would wonder who would pay for the vast networks of roads that would be needed to carry automobiles. Their skepticism would be reinforced by the worries of police officials fearful of motorized thieves evading apprehension, and by the opposition of railroad executives foreseeing the collapse of their passenger business as people abandoned trains for cars.

Energy experts would react in horror at the prospect of supplying the gasoline stations and the vast quantities of petroleum necessary to fuel automobiles which, unlike buses and trucks, would be stored at home and not at a central depot and would burn much more fuel per person carried than some of their mass-transit alternatives.

In short, the automobile, the device on which most Americans rely for not only transportation but mobility, privacy, and fun would not exist if it had to be created today. Of course, the car does exist, and has powerfully affected the living, working, and social spaces of America. But the argument against it persists. That argument dominates the thinking of academic experts on urban transportation and much of city planning. It can be found in countless books complaining of dreary suburban architecture, endless trips to and from work, the social isolation produced by solo auto trips, and the harmful effects of the car on air quality, noise levels, petroleum consumption, and road congestion.

In her recent book, *Asphalt Nation: How the Automobile Took Over America and How We Can Take it Back,* Jane Holtz Kay, the architecture critic for the *Nation,* assails the car unmercifully. It has, she writes, "strangled" our lives and landscape, imposing on us "the costs of sprawl, of pollution, of congestion, of commuting." For this damage to be undone, the massively subsidized automobile will have to be sharply curtailed, by investing heavily in public transportation and imposing European-like taxes on gasoline. (According to Kay, if we cut highway spending by a mere $10 million, we could buy bicycles for all 93,000 residents of Eugene, Oregon, over the age of eleven.) What is more, people ought to live in cities with high population densities, since "for mass transit," as Kay notes, "you need mass." Housing should be built within a short walk of the corner store, and industries moved back downtown.

In Kay's book, hostility to the car is linked inextricably to hostility to the low-density suburb. Her view is by no means one that is confined to the political Left. Thus, Karl Zinsmeister, a conservative, has argued in the *American Enterprise* that we have become "slaves to our cars" and that, by using them to live in suburbs, we have created "inhospitable places for individualism and community life." Suburbs, says Zinsmeister, encourage "rootlessness" and are the enemy of the "traditional neighborhood" with its "easy daily interactions."

The same theme has been taken up by Mark Gauvreau Judge in the *Weekly Standard.* Emerging from his home after a heavy snowfall, Judge, realizing that the nearest tavern was four miles away, concluded that he had to leave the suburbs. He repeats Zinsmeister's global complaint. Suburbanization, he writes, has fed, and sometimes caused, hurried life, the disappearance of family time, the weakening of generational links, our ignorance of history, our lack of local ties, an exaggerated focus on money, the anonymity of community life, the rise of radical feminism, the decline of civic action, and the tyrannical dominance of TV and pop culture over leisure time.

Wow.

These people must live in or near very odd suburbs. The one in which I lived while my children were growing up, and the different ones in which my married daughter and married son now live, are not inhospitable, rootless, isolated, untraditional, or lacking in daily interactions. The towns are small. Life is organized around the family, for which there is a lot of time. Money goes farther for us than for Manhattanites struggling to get their children into the nursery school with the best link to Harvard. Television is less important than in big cities, where the streets are far less safe and TV becomes a major indoor activity. In most cases you can walk to a store. You know your neighbors. There is a Memorial Day parade. People care passionately and argue intensely about school policies and land-use controls. Of course, these are only my personal experiences—but unlike the critics, I find it hard to convert personal beliefs into cosmic generalizations.

Now I live in a suburb more remote from a big city than the one where my children were raised. Because population density is much lower, my wife and I walk less and drive more. But as I write this, my wife is at a neighborhood meeting, where she will be joined by a travel agent, a retired firefighter, a hospital manager, and two housewives who are trying to decide how best to get the city to fix up a road intersection, prevent a nearby land development, and induce our neighbors to prepare for the fire season. On the way back, she will stop at the neighborhood mail station where she may talk to other friends, and then go on to the market where she will deal with people she has known for many years. She will do so by car.

And so back to our theme. Despite the criticisms of Kay and others, the use of the automobile has grown. In 1960, one-fifth of all households owned no car and only one-fifth owned two; by 1990, only one-tenth owned no car and over one-third owned two. In 1969, 80 percent of all urban trips involved a car and only one-twentieth involved public transport; by 1990, car use had risen to 84 percent and public transit use had fallen to less than 3 percent. In 1990, three-fourths or more of the trips to and from work in nineteen out of our twenty largest metropolitan areas were by a single person in an automobile. The exception was the New York metropolitan region, but even there—with an elaborate mass-transit system and a residential concentration high enough to make it possible for some people to walk to work—solo car use made up over half of all trips to work. Some critics explain this American fascination with the car as the unhappy consequence of public policies that make auto use more attractive than the alternatives. To Jane Holtz Kay, if only we taxed gasoline at a high enough rate to repay society for the social costs of automobiles, if only we had an elaborate mass-transit system that linked our cities, if only we placed major restraints on building suburbs on open land, if only we placed heavy restrictions on downtown parking, then things would be better.

Would they? Charles Lave, an economist at the University of California at Irvine, has pointed out that most of Western Europe has long had just these sorts of anti-auto policies in effect. The result? Between 1965 and 1987, the growth in the number of autos per capita has been three times faster in Western Europe than in the United States. Part of the reason for the discrepancy is that the American auto market is approaching saturation: we now have roughly one car in existence for every person of driving age. But if this fact helps explain why the car market here is not growing rapidly, it does not explain the growth in Europe, which is the real story.

Despite policies that penalize car use, make travel very expensive, and restrict parking spaces, Europeans, once they can afford to do so, buy cars, and drive them; according to Lave, the average European car is driven about two-thirds as many miles per year as the average American car. One result is obvious: the heavily subsidized trains in Europe are losing business to cars, and governments there must pay an even larger share of the running cost to keep the trains moving.

In fact, the United States *has* tried to copy the European investment in mass transit. Relentlessly, transportation planners have struggled to find ways of getting people out of their cars and into buses, trains, and subways (and car-pools). Relentlessly, and unsuccessfully. Despite spending about $100 billion, Washington has yet to figure out how to do it.

New subway systems have been built, such as the BART system in San Francisco and the Metro system in Washington, D.C. But BART, in the words of the transportation economist Charles L. Wright, "connects almost nothing to little else." The Metro is still growing, and provides a fine (albeit expensive) route for people moving about the city; but only 7 percent of all residential land area in Washington is within a mile of a Metro station, which means that people must either walk a long way to get to a stop or continue to travel by car. Between 1980 and 1990, while the Washington Metrorail system grew from 30 to 73 miles of line and opened an additional 30 stations, the number of people driving to work increased from 980,000 to 1,394,000, and the transit share of all commutes declined.

The European experience should explain why this is so: if people can afford it, they will want to purchase convenience, flexibility, and privacy. These facts are as close to a Law of Nature as one can get in the transportation business. When the industrial world became prosperous, people bought cars. It is unstoppable.

Suppose however, that the anti-car writers were to win over the vastly more numerous pro-car drivers. Let us imagine what life would be like in a carless nation. People would have to live very close together so they could walk or, for healthy people living in sunny climes, bicycle to mass-transit stops. Living in close quarters would mean life as it is now lived in Manhattan. There would be few freestanding homes, many row houses, and lots of apartment buildings. There would be few private gardens except for flowerpots on balconies. The streets would be congested by pedestrians, trucks, and buses, as they were at the turn of the century before automobiles became common.

Moving about outside the larger cities would be difficult. People would be able to take trains to distant sites, but when they arrived at some attractive locale it would turn out to be another city. They could visit the beach, but only (of necessity) crowded parts of it. They could go to a national park, but only the built-up section of it. They could see the countryside, but (mostly) through a train window. More isolated or remote locations would be accessible, but since public transit would provide the only way of getting there, the departures would be infrequent and the transfers frequent.

In other words, you could see the United States much as most Europeans saw their countryside before the automobile became an important means of locomotion. A train from London or Paris would take you to "the country" by way of a long journey through ugly industrial areas to those rural parts where either you had a home (and the means to ferry yourself to it) or there was a reason (that would be crowded enough to support a nearby train stop).

All this is a way of saying that the debate between car defenders and car haters is a debate between private benefits and public goods. List the charac-teristics of travel that impose few costs on society and, in general, walking, cycling, and some forms of public transit will be seen to be superior. Non-car methods generate less pollution, use energy a bit more efficiently, produce less noise, and (with some exceptions) are safer. But list the characteristics of travel that are desired by individuals, and (with some exceptions) the car is clearly superior. The automobile is more flexible, more punctual, supplies greater comfort, provides for carrying more parcels, creates more privacy, enables one to select fellow passengers, and, for distances over a mile or more, requires less travel time.

As a practical matter, of course, the debate between those who value private benefits and those who insist on their social costs is no real debate at all since people select modes of travel based on individual, not social, prefer-ences. That is why in almost every country in the world, the automobile has triumphed, and much of public policy has been devoted to the somewhat inconsistent task of subsidizing individual choices while attempting to reduce the costs attached to them. In the case of the automobile, governments have attempted to reduce exhaust pollution, make roadways safer, and restrict use (by tolls, speed bumps, pedestrian-only streets, and parking restrictions) in neighborhoods that attach a high value to pedestrian passage. Yet none of these efforts can alter the central fact that people have found cars to be the best means for getting about.

Take traffic congestion. Television loves to focus on grim scenes of grid-locked highways and angry motorists, but in fact people still get to work faster by car than by public transit. And the reason is not that car drivers live close to work and transit users travel a greater distance. According to the best estimates, cars outperform public transit in getting people quickly from their front doors to their work places. This fact is sometimes lost on car crit-ics. Kay, for example, writes that "the same number of people who spend an hour driving sixteen lanes of highway can travel on a two-track train line." Wrong. Train travel is efficient *over a fixed, permanent route,* but people have to find some way to get to where the train starts and get to their final destination after the train stops. The *full* cost of moving people from home to work and back to the home is lower for cars than for trains. Moreover, cars are not subject to union strikes. The Long Island railroad or the bus system may shut down when workers walk off the job; cars do not.

The transportation argument rarely seems to take cognizance of the superiority of cars with respect to individual wants. Whenever there is a discussion about how best to move people about, mass-transit supporters typically overestimate, usually by a wide margin, how many people will leave their cars and happily hop onto trains or buses. According to one study, by Don Pickerell, the vast majority of American rail-transportation proposals greatly exaggerate the number of riders to be attracted; the actual ridership turns out to be about a third of the predicted level. For this reason, urban public transport almost never recovers from the fare box more than a fraction of the actual cost of moving people. Osaka, Japan, seems to be the only large city in the world that gets back from passengers what it spends; in Atlanta, Detroit, and Houston, public transit gets from passengers no more than a third of their cost.

So the real debate ought not be one between car enthusiasts and mass-transit advocates, but about ways of moderating the inevitable use of cars in order to minimize their deleterious effects. One such discussion has already had substantial effects. Auto-exhaust pollution has been dramatically reduced in this country by redesigning engines, changing fuels (largely by removing lead), and imposing inspection requirements.

Since the mid-1960s, auto emissions have been reduced by about 95 percent. Just since 1982, ten years after the Clean Air Act was passed, carbon-monoxide levels have fallen by 40 percent and nitrogen-oxide levels by 25 percent. I live in the Los Angeles area and know from personal experience how irritating smog was in the 1950s. I also know that smog has decreased dramatically for most (but not all) of the region. The number of "smog alert" days called by the South Coast Air Quality Management District (AQMD) declined from 121 in the mid-1970s to seven in 1996. AQMD now predicts that by the year 2000 the number may fall to zero.

Nationally, very little of this improvement has come about from moving people from solo cars into car-pools or onto mass transit—what experts call "Transportation Control Measures" (TCMs)—the combined effect of mass transit, car-pools, telecommuting, and the like—have produced small reductions in smog levels. Transit expansion has decreased carbon monoxide by six-tenths of 1 percent and car pools by another seven-tenths of 1 percent. Adding BART to San Francisco has had only trivial effects on pollution. The Environmental Protection Agency (in the Clinton administration) has issued a report that puts it bluntly: "Efforts to reduce emissions through traditional TCMs have not generated significant air-quality benefits." The methods that *have* reduced pollution significantly are based on markets, not capital investments, and include smog fees, congestion pricing, gas taxes, and higher parking charges.

There is still more pollution to eliminate, but the anti-car enthusiasts rarely approach the task rationally. General Motors now leases electric cars, but they are very expensive and require frequent recharging from scarce power outlets. The electric car is an impressive engineering achievement, but not if you want to travel very far.

We could pass laws that would drive down even further the pollution output of cars, but this would impose huge costs on manufacturers and buyers without addressing the real source of auto pollution—a small percentage of older or modified cars that generate huge amounts of exhaust. Devices now exist for measuring the pollution of cars as they move on highways and then ticketing the offenders, but only recently has there been a large-scale trial of this method, and the results are not yet in. The method has the virtue of targeting enforcement on real culprits, but the defect (for car critics) of not requiring a "tough new law" aimed at every auto owner.

As for traffic congestion, that has indeed become worse—because highway construction has not kept pace with the growth of automobile use. But it is not as bad as some imagine—the average commuting time was the same in 1990 as in 1980—and it is not bad where it is often assumed to be bad. A road is officially called "congested" if its traffic volume exceeds 80 percent of its designed capacity. By this measure, the most congested highways are in and around Washington, D.C., and San Francisco. But if you drive these roads during rush hour, as I have, you will acquire a very different sense of things. The highways into Washington and San Francisco do produce blockages, usually at familiar intersections, bridges, or merges. They rarely last very long and, on most days, one can plan around them.

Indeed, the fact and consequences of auto congestion are greatly exaggerated in most large cities. During rush hour, I have driven into and out of Dallas, Kansas City, Phoenix, St. Louis, and San Diego without much more than an occasional slowdown. Moreover, despite the massive reliance on cars and a short-term decline in the economic vitality of their downtown areas, most of these cities have restored their central areas. Kansas City is bleak in the old downtown, but the shopping area (built 75 years ago!) called Country Club Plaza is filled with people, stores, and restaurants. San Diego and San Francisco have lively downtowns. Los Angeles even managed to acquire a downtown (actually, several downtowns) after it grew up without much of one—and this in a city allegedly "built around the car." Phoenix is restoring its downtown, and San Diego never really lost its center.

Real congestion, by contrast, is found in New York City, Chicago, and Boston, where almost any movement on any downtown street is extremely difficult. From the moment you enter a car or taxi, you are in a traffic jam.

Getting to the airport by car from Manhattan or Boston is vastly more difficult than getting there from San Francisco, Los Angeles, or Washington.

But the lesson in this should be disturbing to car critics: *car travel is most congested in cities that have the oldest and most highly developed rail-based transit systems.* One reason is historical: having subways from their early days, these cities built up to high levels of residential and commercial concentration. A car added to this mix has to navigate through streets surrounded by high office buildings and tall apartment towers. When many people in those buildings take cars or taxis, the congestion can be phenomenal.

But there is another reason as well. Even where rail transportation exists, people will not use it enough to relieve congestion. There is, for example, an excellent rail line from O'Hare Airport to downtown Chicago, and some people use it. But it has done little or nothing to alleviate congestion on the parallel highway. People do not like dragging suitcases on and off trains. And the train does not stop where people want to go—namely, where they live. It stops at busy street corners, sometimes in dangerous neighborhoods. If you take the train, you still must shift to a car at the end, and finding one is not always easy. This is why taking a car from the Los Angeles airport, though it will place you in a few pockets of congestion, gets you to your home faster (and with all of your belongings) than taking a train and taxi a comparable distance from O'Hare.

A great deal can still be done to moderate the social costs of automobile traffic. More toll roads can be built with variable rates that will allow people to drive—at different prices, depending on the level of congestion—to and from cities. Bridges into cities can charge tolls to ensure that only highly motivated people consume scarce downtown road space. (A friend of mine, a distinguished economist, was once asked, in derision, whether he would buy the Brooklyn Bridge. "I would if I could charge tolls on it," he replied.) Cars can be banned from streets that are capable of being pedestrian malls—though there are not many such places. (A number of such malls were created for the purpose of keeping people downtown who did not want to be downtown and were doomed to failure from the start.)

Other measures are also possible. More bicycle pathways can be created, though these are rarely alternatives to auto transportation; some people do ride a bike to work, but few do so often. Street patterns in residential areas can be arranged to minimize the amount of through road traffic they must endure. Gasoline taxes can be set high enough to recover more of the social costs of operating automobiles. (This will not happen in a society as democratic as ours, but it is a good idea, and maybe someday a crisis will create an opportunity.) Portland, Oregon, has become well-known among American cities for having adopted a law—the Urban Growth Boundary— that denies people the right to build almost any new structure in a green belt starting about twenty minutes from downtown. This means that new subdivisions to which one must travel by car cannot be created outside the line.

The nice result is that outside the city, you can drive through unspoiled farmland.

The mayor and downtown business leaders like what they have created. So do environmentalists, social-service organizations, and many ordinary citizens. The policy, described in a recent issue of *Governing* magazine, is called the New Urbanism, and has attracted interest from all over the country. But the policy also has its costs. As the city's population grows, more people must be squeezed into less space. Housing density is up. Before the Urban Growth Boundary, the average Portland house was built on a lot about 13,000 feet square and row houses made up only 3 percent of all dwelling units. Now, the average lot size has fallen to 8,700 square feet, and row houses make up 12 percent of the total. And housing prices are also up. Six years ago, Portland was the nation's 55th most affordable city; today, it is the 165th.

As density goes up in Portland, so will the problems associated with density, such as crime. Reserving land out of a city for scenic value is an important goal, but it must be balanced with supplying affordable housing. Portland will work out the balance, once people begin to yearn for lower density.

But even if we do all the things that can be done to limit the social costs of cars, the campaign against them will not stop. It will not stop because so many of the critics dislike everything the car stands for and everything that society constructs to serve the needs of its occupants.

Cars are about privacy; critics say privacy is bad and prefer group effort. (Of course, one rarely meets these critics in groups. They seem to be too busy rushing about being critics.) Cars are about autonomy; critics say that the pursuit of autonomy destroys community. (Actually, cars allow people to select the kind of community in which they want to live.) Cars are about speed; critics abhor the fatalities they think speed causes. (In fact, auto fatalities have been declining for decades, including after the 55-mile-per-hour national speed limit was repealed. Charles Lave suggests that this is because higher speed limits reduce the variance among cars in their rates of travel, thereby producing less passing and overtaking, two dangerous highway maneuvers.) Cars are about the joyous sensation of driving on beautiful country roads; critics take their joy from politics. (A great failing of the intellectual life of this country is that so much of it is centered in Manhattan, where one finds the highest concentration of non-drivers in the country.) Cars make possible Wal-Mart, Home Depot, the Price Club, and other ways of allowing people to shop for rock-bottom prices; critics want people to spend their time gathering food at downtown shops (and paying the much higher prices that small stores occupying expensive land must charge). Cars make California possible; critics loathe California. (But they loathe it for the wrong reason. The state is not the car capital of the nation; 36 states have more cars per capita, and their residents drive more miles.)

Life in California would be very difficult without cars. This is not because the commute to work is so long; in Los Angeles, according to Charles Lave, the average trip to work in 1994 was 26 minutes, five minutes *shorter* than in New York City. Rather, a carless state could not be enjoyed. You could not see the vast areas of farmland, the huge tracts of empty mountains and deserts, the miles of deserted beaches and forests. No one who visits Los Angeles or San Francisco can imagine how much of California is, in effect, empty, unsettled. It is an empire of lightly used roads, splendid vistas, and small towns, intersected by a highway system that, should you be busy or foolish enough to use it, will speed you from San Francisco to Los Angeles or San Diego. Off the interstate, it is a kaleidoscope of charming places to be alone.

Getting there in order to be alone is best done in one of the remarkably engineered, breathtakingly fast, modern cars that give to the driver the deepest sense of what the road can offer: the beauty of its views, the excitement of command, the passion of engagement.

I know the way. If you are a friend, you need only ask.

James Q. Wilson is Collins professor of management and public policy at UCLA and a frequent contributor to *Commentary*. His most recent book is *Moral Judgment* (BasicBooks).

NOTES

1. United Nations Conference on Environment and Development (UNCED). Declaration of Rio, Rio de Janeiro, Brazil: UN, 1992 (Principle 15).

2. Cranberry affair. *Newsweek,* November 23, 1959: 35.

3. U.S. widens taint check for cranberries. *The New York Times,* November 11, 1959: 1.

4. Cranberry crop facing huge loss. *The New York Times,* November 11, 1959: 1.

5. Mercy Ma! No cranberries. *Life,* November 23, 1959: 28.

6. Weed-killer testing of cranberry crop aided by growers. *The New York Times,* November 12, 1959: 1.

7. Benson won't abandon cranberries on holiday. *The New York Times,* November 11, 1959: 29.

8. Cranberries, please. *Newsweek,* November 30, 1959: 27.

9. The cranberry scare—here are the facts. *U.S. News and World Report,* November 23, 1959: 44–45.

10. Williams in protest. *The New York Times,* November 12, 1959: 20.

11. Hayes, W. *Pesticides Studied in Man.* Baltimore: Williams & Wilkins, 1982: 566.

12. Cranberries and Mr. Fleming. *The New York Times,* November 14, 1959: 44.

13. Pesticide scare worries manufacturers. *The New York Times,* November 22, 1959: 1.

14. *Toxic Terror:* 110–114.

15. Meister, K. *Low-Calorie Sweeteners.* New York: American Council on Science and Health, 1993.

16. Whelan, E. and Stare, F. J. *Panic in the Pantry*. New York: Antheneum, 1975: 151–152.

17. Bitterness about sweets. *The New York Times,* October 17, 1969: 79.

18. Bitter Sweeteners? *Newsweek,* September 29, 1969: 79.

19. *Panic in the Pantry,* 1975: 153.

20. *Panic in the Pantry,* 1975: 154–155.

21. *Panic in the Pantry,* 1975: 155–157.

22. FDA extends ban on sweeteners. *Science,* September 4, 1970: 962.

23. *Panic in the Pantry,* 1975: 155.

24. *Panic in the Pantry,* 1975: 160.

25. *Panic in the Pantry,* 1975: 161.

26. *Panic in the Pantry,* Rev. ed. Buffalo, NY: Prometheus Books, 1992: 145.

27. Meister, K. *Low-Calorie Sweeteners,* New York: American Council on Science and Health, 1993: 18.

28. Whelan, E. and Stare, F. J. *Panic in the Pantry*. Buffalo, NY: Prometheus Books, 1992: 146.

29. Whelan, E. and Stare, F. J. *The 100% All Natural Nutrition Hoax*. New York: Atheneum, 1984: 161.

30. Conversation between Adam Lieberman and Dr. Elizabeth Whelan, January 1996.

31. *Panic in the Pantry,* 1992: 147.

32. *Low-Calorie Sweetener:* 20–21.

33. Havender, W. and Whelan, E. Sweet truth. *Reason,* October 1984: 33–38.

34. *Low-Calorie Sweeteners:* 19.

35. Are Hair Dyes Safe? *Consumer Reports,* August 1979: 456–459.

36. National Cancer Institute, Personal use of hair coloring products. *NCI CancerFax.* National Cancer Institute: August 1, 1996: 1.

37. Gwynne, P., and Copeland, J. B. Household worries, *Newsweek,* October 31, 1977: 109.

38. Zahm, S. H., Weisenburger, D. D., Babbit, P. A., et al. Use of hair coloring products and the risk of lymphoma, multiple myeloma, and chronic lymphocytic leukemia. *American Journal of Public Health,* 1992; 82: 990–997.

39. Newman, J. Hair dye distress. *American Health,* November 1992: 39.

40. Grodstein, F., Hennekens, C. H., Colditz, G. A., et al. A prospective study of permanent hair dye use and hematopoietic cancer. *JNCI,* 1994; 86: 1466–1470.

41. Whelan, E. *Toxic Terror,* 2nd ed. Buffalo, NY: Prometheus Books, 1993: 125–129.

42. *Toxic Terror:* 129–130.

43. *Toxic Terror:* 130–131, 133–134.

44. *Toxic Terror:* 131–132.

45. *Toxic Terror:* 134–140.

46. *Toxic Terror:* 141–142, 144–145.

47. Kirschner, E. Love Canal settlement. *Chemical & Engineering News,* June 27, 1994: 4–5.

48. Reisch, M. Court rejects punitive damages for Love Canal. *Chemical & Engineering News,* March 28, 1994: 7.

49. Love Canal settlement highlights Superfund debate. *Chemical Marketing Reporter,* January 1, 1996: 3.

50. *Toxic Terror:* 69–70.

51. Rosen, J. Much ado about Alar. *Issues in Science and Technology,* 1990; 7:85–90.

52. Smith, K. *Alar Five Years Later.* New York: American Council on Science and Health, 1994.

53. Whelan, E. and Stare, F. J., *Panic in the Pantry.* Buffalo, NY: Prometheus Books, 1992: 4.

54. Whelan, E. *Toxic Terror,* 2nd ed. Buffalo, NY: Prometheus Books, 1993: 198.

55. *Toxic Terror:* 190.

56. *Toxic Terror:* 191–194.

57. *Toxic Terror:* 198.

58. *Toxic Terror:* 194.

59. *Evaluation on Daminozide.* U.K. Ministry of Agriculture, Fisheries and Food, Pesticides Safety Division, 1989.

60. *Toxic Terror:* 199–200.

61. Schneider, K. A policy that set the world standard goes off track. *ECO,* June 1993: 17–22.

62. Marshall, E. A is for Apple, Alar, and . . . alarmist? *Science,* 1991; 254: 20–22.

63. Letter to the editor, *The Wall Street Journal,* March 29, 1996.

64. Negin, E. The Alar 'scare' was real. *Columbia Journalism Review,* September-October, 1996: 13–15.

65. For one example, see: Clamorous pro and con campaign heralds book's launch. *The Wall Street Journal,* March 7, 1996; B1.

66. *Toxic Terror:* 194–196.

67. Campbell, S. Asbestos in schools: how much hazard? *ACSH News and Views,* September/October 1985.

68. Whelan, E. Asbestos in schools: the latest phantom risk. *Priorities,* Fall/Winter 1993: 38.

69. Environmental Defense Fund. The campaign to end use of deadly asbestos. *EDF Letter.* Vol. XIX, No. 3, June 1988: 2.

70. Whelan, E. *Toxic Terror,* 2nd ed. Buffalo, NY: Prometheus Books, 1993: 267–268.

71. *Toxic Terror:* 270–272.

72. EPA tells schools asbestos can stay, but it's too late. *Detroit Free Press,* September 14, 1990: 1.

73. Byron, C. The phony asbestos scare. *New York,* September 15, 1993: 22–23.

74. National Cancer Institute. *Cancer Facts: Questions and Answers About Asbestos Exposure,* November 30, 1995.

75. Campbell, S. Asbestos in schools: How much hazard? *ACSH News and Views,* September/October 1985.

76. National Cancer Institute, *Cancer Facts: Electromagnetic Field Exposure and Cancer Studies at the NCI,* August 1, 1996.

77. Conkling, W. Shocking charges. *American Health,* May 1993: 50–55.

78. Elmer-Dewitt, P. Dialing "P" for panic. *Time,* February 8, 1993: 56.

79. Call at your own risk. *20/20* [television program]. ABC News, Transcript #1305, January 29, 1993.

80. Conkling, W. Shocking charges. *American Health,* May 1993: 50–55.

81. Elmer-Dewitt, P. Dialing "P" for panic. *Time,* February 8, 1993: 56.

82. Moore, M. Jury still out on safety of cellular technology. *PC Week,* February 15, 1993.

83. Ziegler, B. Remember the cellular-phone scare? *Business Week,* July 19, 1993: 83.

84. Conkling, W. Shocking charges. *American Health,* May 1993: 50–55.

85. The cellular phone controversy. *CNN Moneyline* [television program]. Transcript #828, February 2, 1993.

86. Call at your own risk. *20/20* [television program]. ABC News, Transcript #1305, January 15, 1993.

87. Center for Devices and Radiological Health, Food and Drug Administration. Center addresses cellular phone issues. *Radiological Health Bulletin,* Spring 1993; 227: 2–4.

88. Graham, J. D. and Putnam, S. Cellular telephones and brain cancer. *Risk in Perspective.* Harvard Center for Risk Analysis, June 1995; 3: 1–2.

89. Ziegler, B. Remember the cellular-phone scare? *BusinessWeek,* July 19, 1993: 83.

90. International Commission on Non-Ionizing Radiation Protection (ICNIRP). Health issues related to the use of hand-held radiotelephone and base transmitters. *Health Physics,* 1996; 70: 453–458.

91. International Commission on Non-Ionizing Radiation Protection (ICNIRP). Health issues related to the use of hand-held radiotelephone and base transmitters. *Health Physics,* 1996; 70: 453–458.

92. Center for Devices and Radiological Health, Food and Drug Administration. Center addresses cellular phone issues. *Radiological Health Bulletin,* Spring 1993; 227: 2–4.

93. Redelmeier, D. A. and Tibshirani, R. J. Association between cellular-telephone calls and motor vehicle collisions. *N. Engl. J.* ed. 1997; 336: 453–458.

3

Affirmative Action: Is It Justice or a New Prejudice?

Perhaps the most controversial policy involving race is the issue of affirmative action. This is a long-standing policy which started in a small way under President Nixon. The program was greatly expanded under subsequent administrations. It has grown to include hundreds of separate programs at the federal level alone. At the state and local level it includes thousands of programs. The cost to the nation is in the tens of billions of dollars every year.

Two articles by George Zilbergeld challenge the basic assumptions about affirmative action. "Affirmative Action is Immoral and Dangerous" examines some of the damage caused by affirmative action programs, an issue that is often ignored in discussions in the media and on college campuses. The second article by Zilbergeld, "If Racial Preferences Are So Unpopular, Why Are They So Prevalent?" examines the question of why racial preferences continue to roll along like the mighty Mississippi when polls consistently show that most Americans are against them. Why haven't more politicians sought to end affirmative action, especially in its most extreme forms? This article examines the anti-democratic forces and institutions that have played a major role in initiating and maintaining this unpopular practice. On campuses as well as in the political arena, politically correct supporters of affirmative action have squelched debate by portraying anyone who questions the justice or effectiveness of racial preferences as a racist.

In "White Minorities Get Shafted," Dante Ramos lays out the inconsistency and unfairness with which affirmative action guidelines have been applied. He provides persuasive evidence that preferences are often given to groups and individuals who don't need them and denied to those who do. The section concludes with a thought provoking "Affirmative Action Pledge," designed by supporters of preference victim Cheryl Hopwood at the University of Texas, which you should not give to anyone to sign—unless you are rich, very good looking, can run fast, or are planning to drop the courses of professors who claim to support affirmative action.

Reading 13
AFFIRMATIVE ACTION IS IMMORAL AND DANGEROUS
George Zilbergeld

Affirmative action programs provide preferential treatment to groups identified by such characteristics as skin color, ethnicity, or gender. Supporters claim that affirmative action merely levels the playing field or makes up for past injustices. But the most important question is who decides and on what basis they decide who will be today's winners and losers in the racial lottery system.

Affirmative action programs are immoral because they choose winners and losers on a basis having nothing to do with effort or ability. Today's random winners include people who used to live in South America and Africa. Why?

Why should recent arrivals from South America have a better chance of being admitted to a good college or getting a job? Aren't many of the ancestors of the people who come from Latin America the people who originally came from Spain and promptly annihilated the Incas and Aztecs? Why do we reward their descendants?

People with black skin who are recent immigrants from Africa receive special privileges. Why? It is possible to make a rational case for special benefits for black Americans whose ancestors were slaves, but how do you make a rational case for recent arrivals?

What is the proper category if your father came from Mexico and your mother came from England? Should we use a light meter to decide who is a winner?

The group lottery system also produces random losers. In America, there are millions of people whose relatives died in concentration camps, were murdered by the Communists in Russia, or starved to death in Ireland. There are also millions of relatives of soldiers who fought and died for America. These people all become losers because they are without a preferred minority status.

Affirmative action is not only immoral. It is dangerous. Many of the world's trouble spots, such as Yugoslavia, Afghanistan, and Rwanda, are a result of government-supported group identity and group privilege, which led to group hatred and violence. Before we support group preferences, we should stop to ponder the old advice to be careful what you ask for because you might just get your wish. If you ask for government-supported identity and privileges, you might just get them. But what will be the cost?

There are real problems of opportunity and discrimination in our society. The difficulty lies in choosing the proper means to achieve the goal of equality and opportunity for all. To accuse anyone who supports a method other than affirmative action of being a racist is to end the conversation.

History shows that a focus on individual rights yields superior results to a focus on government distribution of benefits to favored groups. Look around the world at the countries that judge people as individuals and those in which the government chooses the winners and losers, according to group identity. Where would you choose to live?

Some will say that, in this country, the government and society have in the past, and continue in the present, to play favorites. Therefore, some say that we should let the government play favorites with those who belong to particular groups that experienced discrimination in the past, but perhaps just for long enough for those left behind to catch up. Others say that once the government starts down this path it will continue to foster prejudice. The government, they say, doesn't change habits easily, and those who receive benefits today will not easily give them up tomorrow. People who favor individual opportunities also say that to play favorites the government would have to have God-like powers to balance one injustice against another. Does, for example, having a parent who died in a concentration camp beat having an entire family that starved to death? What about physical problems? Does blindness top paralysis? If you have black skin but your father is a surgeon, are you more deserving than a white person whose father was a violent drunk? Does the location of your pain play a role? If you were poor in Jamaica, but I was poor in West Virginia, who gets the benefits of affirmative action? Of course there are people who believe that they can decide, but others would say that those who believe that they have the God-like powers to decide are probably the least suited for such a task.

Should we move toward individual opportunities or toward more group privileges?

Reading 14
WHITE MINORITIES GET SHAFTED
Dante Ramos

Suppose your ancestors were ostracized by mainstream American society because they looked different and talked funny. Perhaps they were hounded because of religious or cultural differences. And a generation or more later, your socioeconomic status remains relatively low. Seems like you're a prime candidate for affirmative action assistance. But you're a Pennsylvania German, and you don't make the list.

The Bureau of the Census counts the Pennsylvania Germans as a distinct ancestry group; it includes people who classify their ancestry mainly as Pennsylvania German, Pennsylvania Dutch, Mennonite, or Amish. They can make a claim for affirmative action benefits. David Rempel Smucker, an editor at the Lancaster (Pennsylvania) Mennonite Historical Society, says that in colonial times, English speakers resented the large number of German speakers. And members of the strictest religious groups—the Amish and conservative Mennonites—faced harassment for their pacifism during World War II. According to Census information, the Pennsylvania Germans also have lower mean earnings, $10,339 per year, than the regulars on the affirmative action list: blacks, Native Americans, Hispanics, and Asians. (One percent of Americans received the long questionnaire for the 1990 Census, the data which the Consortium for International Earth Science Information Network in Saginaw, Michigan, stores electronically. Responding were 2,300 Pennsylvania Germans, who represent about 230,000 people.) No one argues that the Pennsylvania Germans suffered from slavery and Jim Crow as blacks did, but neither did, say, Hispanics. They weren't corralled in reservations as Native Americans were, yet neither were Filipinos.

While it may seem facetious to advocate affirmative action for the Pennsylvania Germans, their case raises two questions: Which ethnic groups deserve to be on "the list"—the familiar, albeit uncodified roster of affirmative action beneficiaries? And what criteria determine whether a group is deserving?

The most-cited standard is skin color. Yet as soon as you consider Hispanics, problems arise. Hispanics can be of any race, and 53 percent call themselves white. White Hispanics usually get reclassified in order to make the list. New York City's Department of Business Services, for example, lets businesses owned mainly by Hispanics, along with those by blacks, Native Americans and Asian Americans, bid slightly higher for municipal contracts. These groups benefit since they're all "basically people of color," as spokesperson Jill Mainelli labels them. On the other hand, Spaniards, who are more typically white than are Latin Americans, often don't make the cut. At Carnegie-Mellon University, for instance, Latin Americans get an admissions edge that Spaniards do not.

Some groups, including Hispanic activist groups such as the Mexican American Legal Defense and Education Fund (MALDEF), emphasize persistent discrimination instead of color. According to Kevin Baker, who directs MALDEF's employment program, "The problems of African-Americans in this country and Mexican-Americans are distinct" from those of other groups. On the other hand, Peter Skerry, author of a book about Mexican-American assimilation and a critic of MALDEF, claims that despite longtime suffering, Mexicans now show the same assimilation patterns that other immigrant groups have shown. Census data support Skerry: 31 percent of immigrant Mexican-American adults perform the lowest-paid jobs—service work such as housekeeping and gardening; yet only 14 percent of the native-born Mexican-Americans do. These statistics, among many others, suggest that newcomers start at the bottom of the job ladder and work steadily upward over time.

So maybe list membership really has more to do with socioeconomic status than with any methodical measure of barriers to advancement. Again, check the numbers. According to the 1990 Census, the mean on-the-job earnings for all adults is $15,105. Adult Native Americans earn significantly less, averaging $11,949, and blacks earn a mere $10,912. Hispanics, considered as a group, earn $11,219. At first glance, the standard list makes perfect sense.

But it makes sense only by lumping all Hispanics together and all whites together—and then ignoring high earnings ($16,928) and diversity among Asians. Why do this? These broad rubrics aren't politically or economically cohesive. Mexicans and Cubans, for example, are fiercely independent of one another. Just because Hmongs earn a paltry $3,194, should affluent Chinese or Japanese reap benefits? Why not pull them apart? In some cases that already happens. Spaniards often don't make the Hispanic category because of their European origin. Until the early 1980s, the University of California system excluded all Asian groups except Filipinos from their list. Further splitting, in theory, should create a new, fairer list.

But drawing the line on earnings level presents a challenge. If Argentines, the highest-paid Hispanic group, receive affirmative action benefits, perhaps the list should include every ethnic category less fortunate than they are. In 1990 Argentines earned $15,956 per year on the job. Less successful were the Dutch, Finns, French, Scotch-Irish, Bulgarians, Croats, Slavic Macedonians, Slovenes, Brazilians, Assyrians, Cajuns, and, of course, the Pennsylvania Germans. Of course, none of these groups ever makes the list. On the other hand, the Argentine threshold would disqualify such frequent list-makers as Pakistanis, Sri Lankans, Burmese, Chinese, Japanese, and Asian Indians, whose earnings average $25,198. Other arbitrary income thresholds produce similar problems.

And without even resorting to socioeconomic status, pressure groups are already expanding the list. Politically active Armenians in Pasadena, California, persuaded the City Council in 1985 to give them city set-asides.

Some Arab-American leaders are pressing for assisted status, too. Albert Mokhiber, president of the American-Arab Anti-Discrimination Committee, says his group receives dozens of job discrimination complaints a week and that remedial action might help. "Nobody's saying that these people should stay on special programs forever," he says. "But if [an Arab-American has] been denied loans from a bank because of his national origin, it would help to have an SBA loan."

Past efforts to rid the list-making of politics have often failed. The 1989 Supreme Court decision Croson v. Richmond should have ended lobbying on the municipal level, by requiring that cities and towns justify their contract set-aside lists with hard evidence of discrimination. But, according to Timothy Bates, an economist who studies minority businesses, the only municipal governments that actually conduct the Croson studies are those that favor affirmative action—and they admit a lot of anecdotal testimony to let groups prove discrimination. Smaller groups can get squeezed out. Chicago found so few Native Americans, Bates says, that the city couldn't produce meaningful statistics on them and excluded them from the program.

None of this proves, of course, that affirmative action might not be needed in some cases. For all the fears of those opposed to racial preferences, for example, college-educated black professionals earn $29,441 per year, still far behind whites at $37,383. But if affirmative action is pursued, it surely should be pursued coherently. That means either cutting everybody but blacks and Native Americans off the list (the best option, but one ruled out by other groups' power politics); or ethnic hair-splitting more complex and more elaborate than even the architects of apartheid might have dreamed up. Which is why, of course, many prefer to look the other way. And why the Pennsylvania Germans, among others, have an increasingly persuasive gripe.

Reading 15
IF RACIAL PREFERENCES ARE SO UNPOPULAR, WHY ARE THEY SO PREVALENT?
George Zilbergeld

Although surveys as well as more informal measures of public opinion indicate that racial preferences are unpopular, they remain the practice of the land even when they are not the law of the land. This is because racial preferences work in the shadows of the least democratic institutions in America. Have you ever voted for racial preference? The chances are that neither you nor your democratically elected representatives have done so. Very few laws mandate racial preferences. The support for racial preference comes from judges, academics, and bureaucracies. According to the PC, this is as it should be since America is not a "real" democracy. America, the PC say, may appear to those who lack the secret knowledge to be democratic in form, but in fact everything is run by an economic elite. This elite is also racist, homophobic, and sexist.

This basic idea is inherited from Karl Marx, who called the apparent reality the superstructure of society, and said that below it lay the more important hidden power, which was dominated by an economic elite. The PC have de-emphasized the dominance of economics and placed more emphasis on cultural elements, such as middle-class values, sexual orientation, and gender. The PC believe that the elite is now defined by race (white), class (middle class), gender (male), and sexual orientation (heterosexual). The idea of an elite with superior knowledge, an idea as old as Plato, remains a basic tenet of the PC.

Bureaucracies, especially that of the federal government, are probably the most important element involved in the creation and enforcement of racial preferences. Two federal agencies, the Equal Employment Opportunity Commission (EEOC) and the Office of Federal Contract Compliance (OFCC), lead the movement to discriminate against people who are not members of government-preferred minority groups.

Every single public and private organization that employs more than fifteen people is under the jurisdiction of the EEOC. All can be sued by the EEOC if their work force does not have a proportional representation of the members of government-preferred minority groups. What is the "correct" proportion? Is it the number in your county, state, or nation? You don't know until the EEOC lets you know.

Every single company that *wants* a contract with the federal government (and 400,000 do) must prove to the government that they have a work force that is representative of the relevant work force. What is the relevant work force? The OFCC will let you know. What groups have this advantage? The bureaucracies will let you know. How do you know who belongs to what group? The bureaucracies will let you know. If you belong to a government-preferred group, are you still eligible for privileges after one, two, or three generations of intermarriage? The bureaucracies will let you know.

The federal bureaucracy invented the five preferred minority groups. First the Office of Management and Budget, Statistical Directive 15 created four government-preferred minority groups: American Indian, Asian, Black, and Hispanic. Later, women were added to the list. In some localities other groups have also been added.

The federal bureaucracy also invented the idea of "proportionality." The old definition of discrimination said that it occurred when someone judged a person by their race instead of their individual merits. The federal bureaucracy came up with the idea that a less than proportional number of members of a preferred minority group getting something desirable like admission to a college, jobs as firemen, or in a corporation, meant the government could and would automatically assume that the reason for this lack of proportionality was discrimination. Because of this bureaucratic rule, if you give a test in which members of a government-preferred minority do not do as well as members of the majority, then the government will make the automatic assumption that the reason was discrimination. Your school, company, or state or local government will no longer be eligible for federal funds until you correct this lack of proportionality or "underrepresentation of government-preferred minority groups." As harmful as the denial of funds may be, the government has another weapon—negative publicity. Your company or school will be presented in the media as being intentionally racist or sexist. This may well appear on the front page. Your denial will probably be on page 43 next to the shipping news. After the federal bureaucracy made this rule, whites were considered guilty of racism until proven innocent.

The words "disparate impact" were used to condemn any lack of proportionality and the automatic assumption was that you had intentionally done something that had a bad, i.e., disparate, impact on a government-preferred minority group. You would then be pressured or sued or denied funds until you stopped bringing about the disparate impact.

You could go to court and try to prove that you were not discriminating, but after the Sears Corporation "won" its case fighting against a charge of discrimination at a cost of twenty million dollars, most companies and institutions decided that the better part of valor was to admit guilt and hire by the numbers, giving in to the concept of proportionality.

Just as during the Cold War you could find the most undemocratic countries by looking for those that used words like "democratic republic" in their names, now you can often find organizations that are devoted to undermining equality and opportunity by looking for the words "equal opportunity."

Bureaucracies are most puzzling institutions for many people. They owe much of their power to their complexity and opacity. The founding fathers thought that the main threat to liberty would come from a powerful government, backed by men with guns. A new diffuse threat has instead come forth in a quiet way to dominate our lives in ways never imagined by previous generations. Only recently have both conservatives and liberals begun to awaken to the possibility of rule by bureaucracy.

Alexis De Tocqueville, the Frenchman who observed America in the nineteenth century and brilliantly prophesized its future, is perhaps the best analyst of the shape of bureaucratic things to come. He predicted a new "soft despotism," less harsh but even more pervasive than old-fashioned tyrannies in its power over individuals:

. . . after taking each individual by turns in its powerful hands and kneading him as it likes, the sovereign extends its arms over society as a whole; it covers its surface with a network of small, complicated, painstaking, uniform rules through which the most original minds and the most vigorous souls cannot clear a way to surpass the crowd; it does not break wills, but it softens them, bends them, and directs them; it rarely forces one to act, but it constantly opposes itself to one's acting; it does not destroy, it prevents things from being born; it does not tyrannize, it hinders, comprises, enervates, extinguishes, dazes, and finally reduces each nation to being nothing more than a herd of timid and industrious animals of which the government is the shepherd.[1]

Bureaucracies operate by using a number of devices that are largely off the radar screen of most people. Modern societies need bureaucracies to control very complex societies with very complex rules. Those who spend their entire day writing and enforcing these rules know them better than the average citizen. This kind of specialization is no different from any other kind of legal, medical, or scientific specialization. The people who work full-time in an organization will know the rules better than anyone else will, and they will therefore know and control the flow of information. What information should be collected? If the bureaucracy chooses to collect information regarding the number of Hispanic professors, then, if the number is less than the proportion of Hispanics in the county, state, or country, Hispanics can claim they are "underrepresented." If you are Irish, but the bureaucracies choose not to collect information regarding Irish employment, how can you complain? You don't know how many Irish are employed, and since the bureaucracy doesn't include your category, they will never look to see if you are properly represented.

More fundamentally, bureaucratic rather than democratic legislative decisions are responsible for the abandonment of the American ideal that one should be judged as an individual and not as a member of a group. It is this ideal that has historically deterred groups in America from participating in the kind of ethnic violence so common in other parts of the world. People who might spend much of their time fighting their neighbors if they were back in their native land spend their energy in America trying to get ahead as individuals. Think of how much more peaceful the former Yugoslavia or India or Indonesia would be if less attention were paid to group identity.

The rules passed by the legislative branch of government can never be specific enough for the complexities and ambiguities of everyday life. Only the bureaucracies will be around day-after-day to make all sorts of crucial decisions. For example, did you or your representative have any input in deciding which people are members of government-preferred minority groups? Why not include the Irish? Surely having a quarter of your population starve to death should count as suffering. Why not include the Russian-Americans? Over ten million Russians were murdered by the Russian Communists. Why don't the children of soldiers whose fathers died fighting in Vietnam count? The bureaucrats decide. Ask them. Why should coming from South America get you all the benefits of affirmative action? If you just arrived in this country, when did you suffer in this country—was it at the airport?

The courts joined the bureaucracy in enforcing this idea that whites were guilty until proven innocent and that, therefore, the easiest way around an expensive battle was to go along with constant discrimination against white people. Besides, white people didn't riot and seldom even went to court to defend themselves, apparently believing that if they were called racists they would dissolve into a little pool of liquid. So the bureaucracies backed by the courts continue to rule.

The mass media and academia have also played a role. Most people require the support of others to act upon their feeling that something is wrong. But until recently there was little mention of racial preference, and when affirmative action was mentioned it was in a favorable light, with the implication that anyone opposed was insensitive or worse. Thus any white person who objected to discrimination was in danger of acting alone and being attacked by the liberal media and academics as someone trying to deny members of minorities a fair shake in the world. Any white person who spoke up was in a great danger of being labeled by the media as a racist or at least as racially "insensitive."[2]

Sociologist Alvin Gouldner observed that the politics of welfare state liberalism has become the "official ideology" of wide sectors of the universities: "This political establishment . . . is quite capable of functioning as an 'intellectual Mafia'." Political liberalism today . . . verges on being an official ideology of wide sectors of the American University community as well as broader strata of American life.[3] The power of the liberal establishment in the academic community, which has strongly supported the concept of group entitlement, has tended to isolate and silence many who might otherwise object to preferences and to stigmatize those who do so. Anyone who fights against this major tenet of politically correct ideology will feel the full wrath of the liberal establishment. The combination of the "legal" power of the bureaucracy combined with the propaganda power of the PC establishment explains why group preferences have remained prevalent despite their lack of broad popular support.

During the 1990s there was a major battle over the admission preferences given by the University of Texas School of Law to members of government-preferred minorities such as African Americans and Hispanics. Cheryl Hopwood, a single mother who was raising a severely handicapped child, sued the School of Law when she discovered that African Americans and Hispanics with lower grades and test scores were admitted while she was turned down.

Ms. Hopwood's child died because of medical problems related to his handicapped condition while the case was still in the courts. A federal court eventually stated that the admission system was unconstitutional. While the case was being argued, students supporting Ms. Hopwood circulated the following pledge on campus. There is no record of how many supporters of affirmative action signed the following pledge.

Reading 16
RACIAL PREFERENCES PLEDGE

Dear _____

    I, _____, am a firm supporter of diversity. I understand that under such a system, whites and Asian-Americans will be passed over in favor of members of government-preferred minority groups. I believe that such a system is necessary because of the overarching importance of achieving racial diversity.

    I hereby state that I/my children (circle) as white/Asian-American people (circle), am willing to pay the same costs that race preferences place on others. For this reason I am informing you that I am willing to vacate my/my children's (circle) position as an employee/professor/student (circle) so that a suitable member of a government-preferred minority group member can replace me and my children and contribute to diversity at _____.

    I understand that if I fail to sign this form but continue to say that I support the notion of race preferences/affirmative action/utilization of the underutilized, representation of the underrepresented/diversity that I and my children will be quite rightly be considered *hypocrites*.

    By signing this form, I hereby grant the University/Company (circle one) permission to replace me and my children with a member of a government-preferred minority group. I and my children are willing to be educated/employed at another institution/company for the purpose of promoting greater racial harmony and diversity. Please inform me as soon as my/my children's replacement has been found.

Sincerely,

_____   _____

_____

Signatures

_____   _____

_____

Names (please print)

_____

_____

Social Security numbers

_____

_____

NOTES

1. Alexis DeTocqueville. *Democracy in America*. Translated and edited by Mansfield, Harvey C., and Winthrop, Delba. p. 663. Chicago: Chicago University Press.

2. Quoted in Frederick Lynch. *Invisible Victims: White Males and the Crisis of Affirmative Action.* (New York: Praeger, 1989) pp. 119–120. This book has the best analysis of why so many have been discriminated against and so few have protested.

3. Lynch, 120.

4

War and Veterans: Some Questions for Civilians

Always remember that you sleep at ease at night because rough men stand ready to harm those who would disturb your rest.

—*George Orwell*

Pacifists are among the most immoral of men. They make no distinction between aggression and defense. Therefore, pacifism is one of the greatest allies an aggressor can have.

—*Patrick Henry*

Why are you more likely to see a flying nun on a campus than a military victory celebrated or the sacrifices made by veterans honored? Why are ROTC units often kept off campuses? Why does it require an attack on America before you see a flag on a college campus? Why do the politically correct professors hate to give credit to the military for anything and assume little can be learned by an objective analysis of military history?

In "Arms and the Scholar," Zilbergeld suggests that much can be learned by studying war and the military. The PC have had a far-reaching impact on American attitudes toward the military. Their hostility has influenced the news media and, through them, policy makers who determine military spending and operational guidelines.

Although there is a continuous outcry for diversity on college campuses and in the media, there is little diversity of opinion on public policies, including military policy. Universities frequently lack faculty members with either a background in the military or any expertise in military affairs. At the time of the Gulf War, professor-after-professor said that we would end up in a quagmire, that body bags by the thousands would soon be heading toward America, that the sand would clog our machines, and so on. They were wrong, of course. This continuing lack of expertise may help explain why "peace" rallies on campuses after 9/11 so often featured "experts" drawn from departments of comparative literature or sociology. It may also explain why they were totally wrong in their predictions.

"A Battle Hard Fought, A Victory Delayed" by Wolf Lehmann presents a seldom heard view of the Vietnam War. He suggests that Vietnam was just one battle in a seventy-year war against communism that we eventually won. Is it more reasonable to fail to respect the soldiers who served in Vietnam because it was a battle that we lost than it would be to think less of soldiers who fought in losing battles in World War II or than we do of those who fought in winning battles? The articles by Lehmann and Zilbergeld address these issues. The real facts about the Vietnam War are more complex than the negative images propagated by the politically correct.

Rudyard Kipling's poem "Tommy" dramatizes the contrast between the deference and at least temporary respect shown to soldiers by civilians in time of war and the neglect and disrespect they suffer in peacetime. We have seen a similar shift in attitude since 9/11. However, American soldiers who are fighting now may still wonder how lasting this change will be. How will they be treated when they come home? Will they be ignored and humiliated as were so many Vietnam veterans?

The absence of poems like "Tommy" from current anthologies and syllabi shows the dominance of PC professors on college campuses. Kipling's poems were once among the most popular in the world, but once the PC decided that he was politically unacceptable, his poems quickly disappeared from classrooms.

Since 9/11 we have heard people use the word honor a good deal more than it was used in the past few years. For a while this word seemed to be an old-fashioned term that was rarely heard in public discourse. On 9/11 the entire country witnessed and heard about people of honor. The word *honor* means to act well regardless of the cost or benefit to oneself. When firemen stayed to give comfort to civilians in the World Trade Center, knowing that the civilians were already doomed and that by staying the firemen lost all chance to escape, they did this out of a sense of honor. Perhaps, for a while, the cynics and the PC denied that it existed, and many of us believed them. Fortunately the importance of honor never left the very groups so often denigrated by the politically correct. The PC say that to understand the world you must always ask who benefits. The PC say that certain races, classes, and genders benefit. The actions of some on 9/11 indicate that there are some groups, such as the military and firefighters, who will always do what is right regardless of any other factors. The section on past winners of the military indicates that the importance and worth of honor never left.

Reading 17
TOMMY
Rudyard Kipling

I went into a public-'ouse to get a pint o' beer,
The publican 'e up an' sez, "We serve no red-coats here."
The girls be'ind the bar they laughed an' giggled fit to die,
I outs into the street again an' to myself sez I:

> O it's Tommy this, an' Tommy that, an' "Tommy, go
>   away";
> But it's "Thank you, Mister Atkins," when the band
>   begins to play.

I went into a theatre as sober as could be,
They gave a drunk civilian room, but 'adn't none for me;
They sent me to the gallery or round the music 'alls,
But when it comes to fightin', Lord! they'll shove me in the
    stalls!

> For it's Tommy this, an' Tommy that, an' "Tommy,
>   wait outside";
> But it's "Special train for Atkins" when the trooper's
>   on the tide—
> The troopship's on the tide, my boys, the troopship's
>   on the tide,
> O it's "Special train for Atkins" when the trooper's on
>   the tide.

Yes, makin' mock o' uniforms that guard you while you sleep
Is cheaper than them uniforms, an' they're starvation cheap;
An' hustlin' drunken soldiers when they're goin' large a bit
Is five times better business than paradin' in full kit.

> Then it's Tommy this, an' Tommy that, an' "Tommy,
>   'ow's yer soul?"

> But it's "Thin red line of 'eroes" when the drums begin
> to roll—
> The drums begin to roll, my boys, the drums begin to
> roll,
> O it's "Thin red line of 'eroes" when the drums begin
> to roll.

We aren't no thin red 'eroes, nor we aren't no blackguards too,
But single men in barricks, most remarkable like you;
An' if sometimes our conduck isn't all your fancy paints,
Why, single men in barricks don't grow into plaster saints

> While it's Tommy this, an' Tommy that, an' "Tommy,
> fall be'ind,"
> But it's "Please to walk in front, sir," when there's
> trouble in the wind—
> There's trouble in the wind, my boys, there's trouble
> in the wind,
> O it's "Please to walk in front, sir," when there's
> trouble in the wind.

You talk o' better food for us, an' schools, an' fires, an' all.
We'll wait for extra rations if you treat us rational.
Don't mess about the cook-room slops, but prove it to our face
The Widow's Uniform is not the soldier-man's disgrace.

> For it's Tommy this, an' Tommy that, an' "Chuck him out,
> the brute!"
> But it's "Saviour of 'is country" when the guns begin to
> shoot;
> An' it's Tommy this, an' Tommy that, an' anything you
> please;

An' Tommy ain't a bloomin' fool—you bet that Tommy sees!

Reading 18
ARMS AND THE SCHOLAR
George Zilbergeld

Because of the movie *Saving Private Ryan,* many people in the current generation have learned a little more about military operations and the sacrifices made by veterans. This has caused an outpouring of respect and appreciation for the veterans of World War II. But there is one place where you will hardly ever hear a word of respect or appreciation for the military—college campuses.

I have been offering students extra credit if they see the movie and write a brief review. What comes through is the fact that most students have little understanding of what military action is all about. However, once they see the movie they have a newfound respect for and perspective on the military.

Why are the students so lacking in knowledge of war? Does it matter? I think it does. There are many reasons for college students to learn about war. College graduates tend to be more active in public life, and they will play a larger role in future decisions that involve military action. The decisions they make should be informed decisions. By learning the details of past wars they can make better decisions today.

By studying the Korean War, for example, one learns that American soldiers died because they were not in top physical condition and thus weren't able to go up and down the steep Korean hills fast enough. When you read how American soldiers died after their anti-tank rockets bounced off North Korean tanks, you feel the need to supply our soldiers with the best weapons. When you hear a Korean War veteran talk about how, after he was captured and held in captivity, one of his jobs in the morning was to carry out the American soldiers who had frozen to death during the night, then you gain an appreciation of the sacrifices soldiers make, and you realize that soldiers have to be physically and mentally strong.

Private Ryan also shows the devastating effect of superior equipment in scenes in which the faster and more numerous German machine guns kill scores of Americans. Hopefully, such knowledge will encourage people to think more about military preparedness.

By talking to veterans, students can also learn why wars are terrible but sometimes necessary. Students will not soon forget hearing a veteran from World War II who helped liberate a concentration camp describe what he saw and how grateful the survivors were. They will have an answer to those who say that all wars are a mistake; at the same time exposure to the experience of veterans will insure that we do not go to war for trivial reasons.

I have been a college professor for twenty-five years at three different colleges in three different parts of the United States. I do not remember a single campus-wide celebration or memorial service for the military.

On the other hand there is no lack of criticism of the military. Students have heard numerous debates on whether we should have dropped the atomic bomb on Japan. They have extensively studied the interning of the Japanese Americans during World War II. They have been frequently reminded of the murder of civilians at My Lai. It is necessary for people searching for the whole truth about our country to know about these situations. But their knowledge should also include something of the sacrifices made by veterans.

Wouldn't the students and the faculty (for few faculty have spent time in the military) gain something from hearing directly from the veterans? Why don't we hear more about war and veterans on college campuses? After all, colleges benefit tremendously from the sacrifices made by American soldiers. Who is more dependent on individual liberty than college students and professors?

Why is there such an absolute lack of appreciation and respect shown for veterans on college campuses? Is it because the most energetic and forceful people on campuses are the leftists from the '60s who still view the military as a force for evil in the world? Or is it because, while most professors and administrators do not agree with the far left, many are afraid of being criticized and harassed?

If this is the case, then perhaps it is time to show off a bit of courage on behalf of those to whom we owe so much of our good life, with its personal freedom and prosperity. Feeling respect for characters in a movie such as *Saving Private Ryan* is good. There are many living veterans who wouldn't mind just telling their stories and having other people know the truth. The left needn't worry. Few veterans will glorify war. But meeting veterans and reading about their experiences may help us to appreciate the sacrifices they made and provide us with better ways to judge when we should or should not create more veterans.

Reading 19
A BATTLE HARD FOUGHT, A VICTORY DELAYED
Wolf Lehmann

This reading is a review of *Vietnam: The Necessary War* by Michael Lind.

The struggle for Indochina over some 30 years was an integral part of the global Cold War. That war, lest we forget, was precipitated by Moscow's decision to seize on instability and chaos in the aftermath of World War and to press the Marxist-Leninist agenda under the leadership of the Soviet Union's Communist party.

Such sentiments were rarely spoken without ridicule during the "protest years" of the Vietnam War. And yet they express a geopolitical fact, as Michael Lind reminds us in *Vietnam: The Necessary War.* Mr. Lind is keen to demolish the myths surrounding Vietnam, including the distorted ideas that arose from denying the basic truths of the communist agenda.

During the American debates over Vietnam, Ho Chi Minh and his followers were often portrayed as mere nationalists. But they were first and foremost communists, which meant, among other things, that they were hostile to other Vietnamese nationalists who did not share their totalitarian vision. Indeed, before the U.S. intervention, Ho Chi Minh's cadre had murdered and expelled thousands of Vietnamese who had also sought to end French colonial rule.

Thus Vietnam was not the site of a simple "civil war," as we were so often told. It was, like Korea, a frontline state in a greater contest. As Mr. Lind argues, the failure to resist the Soviet- and Chinese-sponsored takeover of

Indochina in the late 1950s and 1960s would have led to a widespread loss of confidence in U.S. leadership in the region and beyond. Walking away from Vietnam was not a political option for Presidents Kennedy and Johnson—especially in light of the leadership vacuum in Saigon created by the Kennedy administration's ill-considered encouragement of the coup against Ngo Diem in 1963.

So the war was Americanized, and that meant a search for a strategy. President Johnson rightly ruled out a ground invasion of Northern Vietnam, which risked widening the war to a direct military conflict with China. But a blockade of North Vietnamese and Cambodian ports, through which Soviet military equipment reached Hanoi, would *not* have had that result. In short: Haiphong harbor should have been mined long before May 1972.

The initial U.S. strategy of "attrition," using body count as the measure of success, was flawed, as Mr. Lind notes. It proved militarily and politically costly, disproportionate to the effects achieved. Starting in late 1968, "pacification" came into its own. Here the emphasis was on security in rural as well as urban areas, and on giving the population a stake in the economic development of the country. This strategy was increasingly effective.

But on the home front another war was raging, often independent of battlefield realities. Mr. Lind compellingly exposes the workings of the antiwar lobbies. Lenin once dubbed naive Western supporters of the Bolshevik Revolution as "useful idiots." In this sense, there were truly "idiotic" elements in the antiwar campaign, skillfully manipulated by the radical left.

The antiwar campaign continued after American forces had been withdrawn from Vietnam (in 1973) and was intensified in January 1974 as the North Vietnamese began their "final offensive" against the south. The antiwar movement's influence reached high up into the Congress and the media throughout this period. In the summer of 1974, the Saigon correspondent of a major TV network privately confided to me that his New York producers had instructed him not to use the term "communists" to describe the North Vietnamese. Much remains to be brought to light on this subject.

Among the lessons of the Vietnam War, Mr. Lind sees he need to focus our strategy, weapons systems, and force structure on low-intensity conflicts. This is certainly true. I disagree, though, with his notion that future military interventions, at least those analogous to Vietnam, should be undertaken only after determining a "ceiling" on casualties—that is, a number that, when reached, would require us to call it quits. Such a formula would leave an opponent free to manage the conflict on his terms rather than ours.

Mr. Lind criticizes Richard Nixon's attempts to end the war. But the task of returning primary responsibility for the war to the Republic of Vietnam— Nixon's "Vietnamization"—was a noble and proper one. It could not have been completed by 1970, as Mr. Lind suggests. By spring 1972, though, about 500,000 American troops had indeed been withdrawn. More important, the South Vietnamese defeated Hanoi's 1972 "Easter offensive" without

American ground forces (although with U.S. air support). This success did not go completely unnoticed: Nixon's November 1972 landslide electoral victory showed clearly that the public did not buy the arguments of the antiwar movement, whose core element was not satisfied by anything short of a surrender to the communists.

Within weeks of Nixon's resignation in August 1974, Hanoi's policy switched from nibbling away at the 1973 Paris Peace Accords to, in effect, tearing them up. As North Vietnamese Gen. Van Tien Dung revealed in his 1978 book, "Our Great Spring Victory," the loss of political will in Washington shaped Hanoi's decisions. Thus it was decided to move North Vietnamese Army forces through Laos and Cambodia for an assault on the central highlands, with another thrust across the 17th parallel to Hue, Danang, and beyond, converging on Saigon with 16 divisions. In a fit of national impotence imposed by Congress, the U.S. allowed this to happen.

This shameful failure was to create or aggravate problems for American policy in Africa, Central America, and the Middle East for years to come. In the global context of the Cold War, Vietnam was, as Mr. Lind says, a defeat but not a mistake. It was a necessary battle in a war that was finally won when the Berlin Wall came down in 1989.

Wolf Lehmann was American Consul General in the Mekong Delta and Deputy Chief of Mission of the American Embassy in Saigon from 1973 to 1975.

Reading 20
IF KOSOVO AND AFGHANISTAN ARE JUST CAUSES, WHY WASN'T VIETNAM?
George Zilbergeld

Many people who believe that good intentions have guided our actions in Kosovo and Afghanistan still seem reluctant to ascribe good intentions to our actions in Vietnam. Is the difference just a question of whether we win or lose?

The two reasons most often given for engaging in military action are protecting our national interests and backing our moral convictions with action. As a nation we will always face the issue of whether to use force and how much force to use.

In Kosovo, it was difficult to make the argument of national interest. Analogies with Nazi Germany are silly. Serbia, the aggressor, is a small, poor country without the ability to conquer a large portion of the world.

The only possible reason for going to war in Kosovo was humanitarian concern. The heartbreaking pictures of devastated refugees and the stories of widespread murder had an effect on every decent person. The events of September 11th provided the reason for going into Afghanistan. The pictures of smiling women, now free from Taliban tyranny, confirmed that we made the right decision.

So how do these crises compare with Vietnam? A good case can be made that both national and humanitarian interests were at stake in Vietnam. At the time, communism was a murderous totalitarian force that included a super-power with nuclear missiles aimed at us. A strong case could be made that it was in our national interest to stop the communist expansion before they became even more powerful.

An excellent case for intervention in Vietnam also could be made on humanitarian grounds. We had proof that the communists had murdered well over fifty million people, including over fifty thousand in North Vietnam after they consolidated their rule there. We fought a seventy-year war against the communists with both diplomacy and guns. We fought to a tie in Korea. We lost in Vietnam. After seventy years, we won the war when communism collapsed. All the soldiers, not just those who fought the winning battles, deserve to be honored. If it is a good idea to help people in Kosovo or Afghanistan, then why wasn't it a good idea to try to help people in Vietnam? One may find fault with our tactics, but it is harder to impugn our motives. If we acknowledge that good motives drive us to help people in distress now, why do we fail to recognize the good motives that led us to try to help the South Vietnamese?

This is not water under the bridge. In this world, water is always pouring over the bridge. There will be other Kosovos and other Afghanistans. The dilemma is that sometimes when we act to back up our moral convictions, we win, as in World War II, and sometimes we lose and get slandered as well, as in Vietnam.

It is ironic that many of those who protested the Vietnam War, criticizing the motives as well as the actions of the United States, have been so enthusiastic about our efforts in Kosovo. The soldiers who fought in Vietnam should be honored, just as should those who have saved the people of Kosovo and Afghanistan. In both cases, we will be honoring soldiers who made a great sacrifice to help people in need and protect our nation.

Reading 21
MEN OF HONOR

This reading is an excerpt from the U.S. Army Center of Military History's Web site.

THE MEDAL OF HONOR

A medal for individual valor was proposed early in the Civil War, and it was signed into law by President Abraham Lincoln in 1861. The measure provided for awarding a medal of honor "to such noncommissioned officers and privates as shall most distinguish themselves by their gallantry in action, and other soldier-like qualities, during the present insurrection." Congress made the Medal of Honor a permanent decoration in 1863. Almost 3,400 men and one woman have received the award for heroic actions in the nation's battles since that time. The action has to be seen by at least two eyewitnesses, involve the risk of life, and go beyond ordinary bravery. Only one-third of the recipients lived to personally receive the award.

Civil War

Benjamin F. McAlwee

Rank and organization: Sergeant, Company D, 3d Maryland Infantry. Place and date: At Petersburg, Va., 30 July 1864. Birth: Washington, D.C. Date of issue: 4 April 1898.

Citation: Picked up a shell with burning fuse and threw it over the parapet into the ditch, where it exploded; by this act he probably saved the lives of comrades at the great peril of his own.

World War I

Deming Bronson

Rank and organization: First Lieutenant, U.S. Army, Company H, 364th Infantry, 91st Division. Place and date: Near Eclisfontaine, France, 26–27 September 1918. Born: 8 July 1894, Rhinelander, Wis.

Citation: For conspicuous gallantry and intrepidity above and beyond the call of duty in action with the enemy. On the morning of 26 September, during the advance of the 364th Infantry, 1st Lt. Bronson was struck by an exploding enemy hand grenade, receiving deep cuts on his face and the back of his head. He nevertheless participated in the action which resulted in the capture of an enemy dugout from which a great number of prisoners were taken. This was effected with difficulty and under extremely hazardous conditions because it was necessary to advance without the advantage of cover and, from an exposed position, throw hand grenades and phosphorous bombs to compel the enemy to surrender.

On the afternoon of the same day he was painfully wounded in the left arm by an enemy rifle bullet, and after receiving first aid treatment he was directed to the rear. Disregarding these instructions, 1st Lt. Bronson remained on duty with his company through the night although suffering from severe pain and shock. On the morning of 27 September, his regiment resumed its attack, the object being the village of Eclisfontaine. Company H, to which 1st Lt. Bronson was assigned, was left in support of the attacking line, Company E being in the line. He gallantly joined that company in spite of his wounds and engaged with it in the capture of the village. After the capture he remained with Company E and participated with it in the capture of an enemy machine gun, he himself killing the enemy gunner. Shortly after this encounter the company was compelled to retire due to the heavy enemy artillery barrage. During this retirement 1st Lt. Bronson, who was the last man to leave the advanced position, was again wounded in both arms by an enemy high-explosive shell. He was then assisted to cover by another officer who applied first aid. Although bleeding profusely and faint from the loss of blood, 1st Lt. Bronson remained with the survivors of the company throughout the night of the second day, refusing to go to the rear for treatment. His conspicuous gallantry and spirit of self-sacrifice were a source of great inspiration to the members of the entire command.

World War II

Seymour W. Terry (medal given posthumously)

Rank and organization: Captain, U.S. Army, Company B, 382d Infantry, 96th Infantry Division. Place and date: Zebra Hill, Okinawa, Ryukyu Islands, 11 May 1945. Birth: Little Rock, Ark.

Citation: 1st Lt. Terry was leading an attack against heavily defended Zebra Hill when devastating fire from 5 pillboxes halted the advance. He braved the hail of bullets to secure satchel charges and white phosphorus grenades, and then ran 30 yards directly at the enemy with an ignited charge to the first stronghold, demolished it, and moved on to the other pillboxes, bombarding them with his grenades and calmly cutting down their defenders with rifle fire as they attempted to escape. When he had finished this job by sealing the 4 pillboxes with explosives, he had killed 20 Japanese and destroyed three machine guns. The advance was again held up by an intense grenade barrage, which inflicted several casualties. Locating the source of enemy fire in trenches on the reverse slope of the hill, 1st Lt. Terry, burdened by 6 satchel charges launched a one-man assault. He wrecked the enemy's defenses by throwing explosives into their positions, and he accounted for 10 of the 20 hostile troops killed when his men overran the area.

Pressing forward again toward a nearby ridge, his two assault platoons were stopped by slashing machine gun and mortar fire. He fearlessly ran across 100 yards of fire-swept terrain to join the support platoon and urge it on in a flanking maneuver. This thrust, too, was halted by stubborn resistance. 1st Lt. Terry began another one-man drive, hurling grenades upon the strongly entrenched defenders until they fled in confusion, leaving 5 dead behind them. Inspired by this bold action, the support platoon charged the retreating enemy and annihilated them. Soon afterward, while organizing his company to repulse a possible counterattack, the gallant company commander was mortally wounded by the burst of an enemy mortar shell. By his indomitable fighting spirit, brilliant leadership, and unwavering courage in the face of tremendous odds, 1st Lt. Terry made possible the accomplishment of his unit's mission and set an example of heroism in keeping with the highest traditions of the military service.

Korean War

William F. Lyell (medal given posthumously)

Rank and organization: Corporal, U.S. Army, Company F, 17th Infantry Regiment, 7th Infantry Division. Place and date: Near Chup'a-ri, Korea, 31 August 1951. Birth: Hickman County, Tenn.

Citation: Corporal Lyell, a member of Company F, distinguished himself by conspicuous gallantry and outstanding courage above and beyond the call of duty in action against the enemy. When his platoon leader was killed, Corporal Lyell assumed command and led his unit in an assault on strongly fortified enemy positions located on commanding terrain. When his platoon came under vicious, raking fire which halted the forward movement, Corporal Lyell seized a 57-millimeter recoilless rifle and unhesitatingly moved ahead to a suitable firing position from which he delivered deadly accurate fire completely destroying an enemy bunker, killing its occupants. He then returned to his platoon and was resuming the assault when the unit was again subjected to intense hostile fire from 2 other bunkers.

Disregarding his personal safety, armed with grenades he charged forward hurling grenades into one of the enemy emplacements, and although painfully wounded in this action he pressed on destroying the bunker and killing six of the foe. He then continued his attack against a third enemy position, throwing grenades as he ran forward, annihilating four enemy soldiers. He then led his platoon to the north slope of the hill where positions were occupied from which effective fire was delivered against the enemy in support of friendly troops moving up. Fearlessly exposing himself to enemy fire, he continuously moved about directing and encouraging his men until he was mortally wounded by enemy mortar fire. Corporal Lyell's extraordinary heroism, indomitable courage, and aggressive leadership reflect great credit on himself and are in keeping with the highest traditions of the military service.

Vietnam

Roy P. Benavidez

Rank and Organization: Master Sergeant, Detachment B-56, 5th Special Forces Group, Republic of Vietnam. Place and Date: West of Loc Ninh on 2 May 1968. Birth: 5 August 1935, DeWitt County, Cuero, Texas.

Citation: Master Sergeant (then Staff Sergeant) Roy P. Benavidez United States Army, who distinguished himself by a series of daring and extremely valorous actions on May 2, 1968 while assigned to Detachment B56, 5th Special Forces Group (Airborne), 1st Special Forces, Republic of Vietnam. On the morning of May 2, 1968, a 12-man Special Forces Reconnaissance Team was inserted by helicopters in a dense jungle area west of Loc Ninh, Vietnam to gather intelligence information about confirmed large-scale enemy activity. This area was controlled and routinely patrolled by the North Vietnamese Army. After a short period of time on the ground, the team met heavy enemy resistance, and requested emergency extraction. Three helicopters attempted extraction, but were unable to land due to intense enemy small arms and anti-aircraft fire. Sergeant Benavidez was at the Forward Operating Base in Loc Ninh monitoring the operation by radio when these helicopters returned to off-load wounded crew members and to assess aircraft damage.

Sergeant Benavidez voluntarily boarded a returning aircraft to assist in another extraction attempt. Realizing that all the team members were either dead or wounded and unable to move to the pickup zone, he directed the aircraft to a nearby clearing where he jumped from the hovering helicopter, and ran approximately 75 meters under withering small arms fire to the crippled team. Prior to reaching the team's position he was wounded in his right leg, face, and head. Despite these painful injuries, he took charge, repositioning the team members and directing their fire to facilitate the landing of an extraction aircraft, and the loading of wounded and dead team members. He then threw smoke canisters to direct the aircraft to the team's position.

Despite his severe wounds and under intense enemy fire, he carried and dragged half of the wounded team members to the awaiting aircraft. He then provided protective fire by running alongside the aircraft as it moved to pick up the remaining team members. As the enemy's fire intensified, he hurried to recover the body and classified documents on the dead team leader. When he reached the leader's body, Sergeant Benavidez was severely wounded by small arms fire in the abdomen and grenade fragments in his back. At nearly the same moment, the aircraft pilot was mortally wounded, and his helicopter crashed.

Although in extremely critical condition due to his multiple wounds, Sergeant Benavidez secured the classified documents and made his way back to the wreckage, where he aided the wounded out of the overturned aircraft, and gathered the stunned survivors into a defensive perimeter. Under increasing enemy automatic weapons and grenade fire, he moved around the perimeter distributing water and ammunition to his weary men, reinstilling in them a will to live and fight. Facing a buildup of enemy opposition with a beleaguered team, Sergeant Benavidez mustered his strength, began calling in tactical air strikes and directed the fire from supporting gunships to suppress the enemy's fire and so permit another extraction attempt. He was wounded again in his thigh by small arms fire while administering first aid to a wounded team member just before another extraction helicopter was able to land. His indomitable spirit kept him going as he began to ferry his comrades to the craft.

On his second trip with the wounded, he received additional wounds to his head and arms before killing his adversary. He then continued under devastating fire to carry the wounded to the helicopter. Upon reaching the aircraft, he spotted and killed two enemy soldiers who were rushing the craft from an angle that prevented the aircraft door gunner from firing upon them. With little strength remaining, he made one last trip to the perimeter to ensure that all classified material had been collected or destroyed, and to bring in the remaining wounded. Only then, in extremely serious condition from numerous wounds and loss of blood, did he allow himself to be pulled into the extraction aircraft. Sergeant Benavidez's gallant choice to join voluntarily his comrades who were in critical straits, to expose himself constantly to withering enemy fire, and his refusal to be stopped despite numerous severe wounds, saved the lives of at least eight men. His fearless personal leadership, tenacious devotion to duty, and extremely valorous actions in the face of overwhelming odds were in keeping with the highest traditions of the military service, and reflect the utmost credit on him and the United States Army.

5

The Culture Wars: Why Should You Care?

This chapter deals with the philosophical origins of the PC movement and explains how this movement has affected the lives of most Americans. John Fonte's "Why There is a Culture War" explains the Marxist origins of the PC movement. Many people believe that Marxism is dead and buried except for some diehards in Russia. Unfortunately this is far from true. While the belief in the need for a violent revolution is gone, the belief in the need to overthrow the ideals of Western civilization, especially the ideal of liberty, and substitute the ideal of equality, lives on. The belief that the proper path of mankind can only be seen by those who agree with the politically correct elite is alive and well, as is the belief that the ends justify the means.

"Like Multiculturalism? You'll Love Yugoslavia," by George Zilbergeld explains the results of accepting the argument that all cultures are the same. It will prove difficult to name the enemy and fight the war against terrorism if you try to maintain that all cultures are the same.

In "Life, Liberty, and Property," Richard Pipes analyzes the relation of private property and liberty. The PC say that property rights are often in conflict with what they call "human rights," but according to Pipes, property *is* a human right and without it there has never been and there never will be a significant amount of liberty. This could help explain why the PC does not like a capitalist system. For many people, capitalism is just liberty in the economic realm, with all of liberties, benefits, and foibles. For the PC, capitalism is one of the most important sources of evil in the world.

"Why the Middle Class is the Key to Winning the Political Correctness War," by Zilbergeld explains why the middle class may well play such an essential role in defending liberty against the plans of the PC. In colleges, the middle class is one of the groups most likely to be vilified in classrooms. Years ago it was widely taught that having a large middle class was essential for having a free and democratic society. This remains true today, and it is precisely why the PC have such a fear and hatred of the middle class.

After you read "The 'Banality of Evil' and the Political Culture of Hatred," you should ask whether the attitudes toward good and evil held by many intellectuals such as professors and news people are adequate to the tasks faced by this nation since 9/11. Do you think that evil is banal? Professor Hollander's article leads to a number of questions. Some people think that morals are not universal, but are just made up by the powerful at any particular time in history to protect their interests. The particular interests of the powerful, the PC say, are determined mainly by a person's race, class, and gender. But this view might pose some problems. If there is no universal morality, how do you condemn slavery or lack of equality? The PC teach that there is no morality fixed throughout time for all of humanity. After 9/11 some have questioned this relativistic view of morality. If there is no universal morality, then isn't the view of the terrorists as valid as the view of those who fight against the terrorists? Is terror just in the eye of the beholder? Since it now appears that the war against terror will be a long one, this could be a very important question. What is your view?

Reading 22
LIKE MULTICULTURALISM? YOU'LL LOVE YUGOSLAVIA
George Zilbergeld

As a professor I have watched the theory of multiculturalism spread across the educational landscape. From kindergarten to graduate school, everyone in charge of educational policy seems to advocate multiculturalism. Colleges in New Jersey now have multicultural requirements either as particular courses or as components of traditional courses.

But before we rush any further along this path it might be worthwhile to think about what we mean by multiculturalism and consider some possible consequences. After all, educational policy is strewn with fads that once elicited great enthusiasm but have few supporters today. For example, does anyone remember with fondness the "open classroom," "team teaching," or the "new math"?

Multiculturalism is often touted as a shorthand for tolerance and respect for other cultures. The assumption is made that if you are not supportive of multiculturalism, you must be intolerant and disrespectful of other cultures.

There is no doubt that we should be tolerant of other cultures and celebrate their accomplishments. But if multiculturalism is interpreted to mean that all cultures are equally worthy of celebration, perhaps we should be more cautious. If all cultures are equal, how can we condemn slavery, dictatorship, and intolerance? If all cultures are equal, then cultures that embrace these practices are as valid as those that condemn slavery and celebrate liberty and tolerance.

There are two aspects of culture. One involves private choices such as how you dress and what you use to season your food. At this level, all cultures are equal. The other aspect of culture involves the public or civic culture. Our civic culture judges people as individuals, not as members of a group. It is precisely this element of our civic culture that makes it possible for different people in this country to live together. Does this make our culture superior? That depends. Do you believe that tolerance, democracy, and liberty are morally superior to intolerance and dictatorship?

While we do have conflicts between groups in this country, most people live in relative harmony with one another. People who used to fight with their neighbors in their native lands do not do so in America. Why aren't the English and the Irish or the Serbs and the Bosnians killing each other in America? The reason is that we have a civic culture that supports tolerance and judges people as individuals. This removes the incentive to organize and hate as members of a group. A civic culture that supports group identity may soon support group hatred, and the country may come to resemble Yugoslavia.

Look at the newspaper and see how the "new tribalism" has brought about endless bloodshed. Read of the "bloody feud between Armenians and Azerbaijanis" and the "50 corpses that lay across from the hospital in Vukovar, Yugoslavia." Read that "Sikh militants kill 20 in India." Read of "residents of North Bombay, India, fleeing from their burning home after it was set on fire by rioters as religious violence between Hindus and Muslims continued." Read how "Kenya, a land that thrived, is now caught up in fear of ethnic civil war."

This country has more people from different groups and backgrounds than any other country. Do we really want to encourage the group identity that led so many people to flee their native lands and come to America, where they could enjoy the benefits of being part of a culture where they would be judged as individuals?

All cultures are not equal. People from all over the world know this. That is why they tunnel under the earth, pay tens of thousands of dollars, enter into fake marriages, and hide in the bottom of dank ships for months to come to this culture. Many of the people who know a great deal about other cultures decide that the best thing they can do is leave and come to America. If they can't get in here, then they might try Canada or Western Europe. If the culture of America and the West are not superior, then why do so many want to come here?

Many of the professors who teach "multiculturalism" actually seem to be a good deal more interested in debasing America and Western civilization than they do in truly learning about other cultures. They accuse those who attribute any type of superiority to America of being racists. But it is not racist to believe that our culture is superior in particular ways. Racism is the belief that superiority has a physical basis such as skin color. Nor does the belief that this is a superior culture mean that all aspects of our cultural are superior. And this certainly does not mean that we have always lived up to our ideals. Indeed, every time we have strayed from the ideal of judging people as individuals, we have experienced horrors such as slavery and bigotry.

However, if we come to think that our cultural values are not superior, then we will cease to defend these values. This would be a very sad situation for those of us who live here and those who wish to come here from other cultures, so that they and their children can experience what they believe is a very special culture indeed. A country that ceases to defend the superiority of a culture that judges the value of people as individuals will soon look very much like Yugoslavia.

Reading 23
LIFE, LIBERTY, PROPERTY
Richard Pipes

As the 20th century draws to a close, the traditional threats to liberty no longer loom large. The downfall of communism has eliminated the most direct and dangerous challenge, while the economic failures of socialism have discredited the notion that the abolition of private ownership in the means of production solves all social ills. Even though tyrannies still manage to hang on to power here and there, they are either isolated or else slowly yielding to the spirit of the times: the slogans of the day are democracy and privatization.[1]

Yet these welcome changes by no means signify that liberty's future is secure: it is still at peril, although from a different and novel source. The main threat to freedom today comes not from tyranny but from equality— equality defined as identity of reward. Related to it is the quest for security.

Liberty is by its nature inegalitarian, because living creatures differ in strength, intelligence, ambition, courage, perseverance, and all else that makes for success. Equality of opportunity and equality before the law—in the sense laid down to the Israelites through Moses in Leviticus 24:22: "Ye shall have one manner of law, as well for the stranger as for the home-born; for I am the Lord your God"—are not only compatible with liberty but essential to it. Equality of reward is not. Indeed, it is attainable only by coercion, which is why all utopian schemes presuppose despotic authority and all despots insist on the equality of their subjects. As Walter Bagehot observed over a century ago, "there is no method by which men can be both free and equal."

Ironically, the enforcement of equality destroys not only liberty but equality as well, for as the experience of communism has demonstrated, those charged with implementing social equality claim for themselves privileges that elevate them high above the common herd. It also results in pervasive corruption, inasmuch as the elite that monopolizes goods and services—as must be done if those goods and services are to be equitably distributed— expects, in return for distributing them, rewards for itself.

And yet the ideal of a Golden Age when all were equal because there was no "mine and thine" has never ceased to appeal to humanity: it is one of our persistent and seemingly indestructible myths. In contrast between equality and liberty, the former holds the stronger hand, because the loss of liberty is felt only when it occurs, whereas the pain of inequality rankles every moment of the day.

The trend of modern times appears to indicate that citizens of democracies are willing heedlessly to surrender their freedoms to purchase social equality (along with economic security), apparently oblivious of the consequences. And the consequences are that their ability to hold on to and use what they earn and own, to hire and fire at will, to enter freely into contracts, and even to speak their mind is steadily eroded by governments bent on redistributing private assets and subordinating individual rights to group rights. Despite the commendable reforms of recent years in the Unites States, the entire concept of the welfare state as it has evolved in the second half of the 20th century stands in tension with individual liberty, for it allows various groups with common needs to combine and claim the right to satisfy them at the expense of society at large, in the process steadily enhancing the power of the state that acts on their behalf.

This reality is currently masked by the immense wealth generated by the industrial economies operating on a global scale in time of peace. It could become painfully apparent, however, should the economic situation drastically deteriorate and the controls established by the state in time of prosperity enable it to restore social stability at the cost of freedom.

Returning the responsibilities for social assistance to the family or private charities, which shouldered them prior to the 20th century, would undoubtedly go a long way toward resolving this predicament. But such a radical solution is neither feasible nor desirable. The libertarian ideal of a society in which the government runs nothing is as unrealistic as the utopian ideal of one in which it runs everything. Even at the height of laissez-faire, government everywhere intervened in some measure in economic and social affairs: the notion of a passive state is as much a myth as that of primitive communism.

This does not mean, however, that it is impossible to find a sensible alternative to the two extreme positions. In dealing with the scope of state power, the question is not either/or—either none or all-embracing—but more or less. When, in the 19th century, the Supreme Court found it necessary to intervene in private contractual engagements—and it did so with great reluctance—the interference was often accompanied by the cautionary adjective "reasonable." Today, although the state must regulate more than ever, such caution is correspondingly more necessary than ever. It must be remembered that the economic rights of citizens (rights to property) are as essential as their civil rights (rights to equal treatment), and that, indeed, the two are inseparable.

Although the concept of human nature has fallen into disfavor, it is difficult to escape the conclusion that there do indeed exist certain constants in human behavior. One of these constants, impervious to legislative and pedagogic manipulation, is acquisitiveness.

In and of itself, the desire to possess manifests greed no more than the appetite for food manifests gluttony, or love lechery. Acquisitiveness is common to all living things, being universal among animals and children as well as adults at every level of civilization. On the most elementary level, it is an expression of the instinct of survival. But beyond this, it constitutes a basic trait of the human personality, for which achievements and acquisitions are means of self-fulfillment. And since fulfillment of the self is the essence of liberty, liberty cannot flourish when property and the inequality to which it gives rise are forcibly eliminated.

In addition to being the most important of liberties, acquiring property is the universal engine of prosperity. The close relationship between property and prosperity is demonstrated by the course of history. Although property in personal belongings is well-nigh universal and known since the dawn of humanity, the ownership of agricultural land—the principal source of livelihood until very modern times—originated in ancient Greece and Rome, and since the Middle Ages spread to the rest of Europe and regions populated by Europeans. One of the main reasons for the rise of the West to its position of global economic preeminence lies in this institution of property, which in much of the rest of the world has led and still leads a rather precarious existence.

The indispensability of property for prosperity can be demonstrated empirically for the contemporary world. The results are impressive in their consistency. Countries that provide the firmest guarantees of economic independence, including private property rights, are virtually without exception the richest. They also enjoy the best civil services and judicial institutions. Today this holds true not only for countries populated by Europeans but also for Japan, South Korea, Hong Kong, Chile, and Taiwan. Conversely, countries that rate lowest in terms of property rights and market freedom— Cuba, Somalia, and North Korea, for instance—languish at the bottom of the scale.

The relationship of property to freedom is more complex, because unlike prosperity, "freedom" has more than one meaning. Thus it is possible to enjoy firm property (economic) rights without political rights, that is, the right to vote. In Western Europe, property rights were respected long before citizens were granted the franchise. Today, some of the most prosperous countries (Singapore, Hong Kong, Taiwan) with the firmest guarantees of property are run in an authoritarian fashion.

It is a serious mistake, unfortunately often committed by the U.S. government in its foreign dealings, to define freedom to mean exclusively democracy, for ordinary citizens may enjoy a wide range of economic and legal freedoms along with personal rights without being able to choose their government. The mistake is probably due to the fact that Americans, as heirs and beneficiaries of English constitutional development, take such freedoms and rights so much for granted that they identify freedom with representative government. The historical evidence indicates that property can coexist with arbitrary and even oppressive political power. Democracy, however, cannot do without it.

The symbiotic relationship between property and freedom does not preclude the state from imposing reasonable restraints on the uses made of objects owned, or ensuring the basic living standards of the neediest strata of the population. Clearly, one cannot allow property rights to serve as a license for ravaging the environment or ignoring the fundamental needs of the unemployed, sick, and aged. Hardly anyone contests this proposition today: even Friedrich Hayek, an implacable foe of state intervention in the economy, agreed that the state has the duty to ensure for all citizens "a minimum of food, shelter, and clothing, sufficient to preserve health and the capacity to work."

But to say this is not to grant the state the authority to use the powers at its disposal to interfere with the freedom of contract, to redistribute wealth on a large scale, or to compel one part of the population to bear the costs of the government-defined "rights" of special constituencies. This is precisely the situation we now face, in particular in the form of limitations on the use of property imposed by various environmental or zoning laws and regulations.

Such limitations should surely be interpreted as "takings" under the Fifth Amendment and adequately compensated. Unfortunately, as the political scientist William Riker has written, this runs counter to the entrenched attitude of the highest organs of the judiciary, which since the late 1930s have assumed "that civil rights and property rights can be sharply distinguished, and that civil rights . . . merit greater judicial protection than property rights."[2] Yet only by a redress of the balance—through court decisions and deregulatory rulings of the government—can the rights of ownership be restored to their proper place in the scale of values instead of being sacrificed to the unattainable ideal of social equality and all-embracing economic security.

Not only do "civil" and "property" rights need to be balanced if we care about freedom, but the whole concept of civil rights requires reexamination. The Civil Rights Act of 1964 gave the government no license to set quotas for hiring personnel in private enterprise or for admitting students to institutions of higher learning; and yet for decades the federal bureaucracy has acted as if it had. Even less did the Act authorize interference with freedom of speech in the workplace in matters of so-called "sexual harassment." But even as property rights have been steadily narrowed in application, the category of "civil rights" has been broadened to include the claims of any group—women, minorities, the disabled, and so forth—to goods and services that fellow citizens must pay for either by sacrificing some of their own rights or else by footing the bill.

The plain truth is that the so-called "social rights" of today, having been bestowed by legislative fiat, are not "rights" in any meaningful sense and certainly not "entitlements," since no one is entitled to anything at someone else's expense; they are, rather, claims on society that it may or may not grant. Nevertheless, in the name of such spurious rights, a large number of citizens in modern industrial democracies are now required to work for the support of others.

In Sweden, the most retrograde state in this respect, for each citizen who earns his own living, 1.8 other citizens are fully or partially maintained by taxes that he is required to pay; in Germany and Great Britain, the ratio is 1:1, and in the U.S., 1:0.76. Because the population dependent on the state includes a heavy proportion of the elderly while the taxpayers are younger wage and salary earners, an unhealthy generational conflict may well develop in welfare societies as the population ages. We see glimmerings of such a conflict in the current dispute in this country over Social Security.

Unless the greatest care is exercised in protecting the rights to property, we may well end up with a regime that, without being tyrannical in the customary sense of the word, is nevertheless unfree. The framers of the American Constitution did not anticipate this possibility: in the words of the 20th-century jurist Roscoe Pound, "They intended to protect the people against their rulers, not themselves." But, as it has turned out, under conditions of modern, welfare-oriented democracy, the threat to liberty can also emanate from one's fellow citizens, who, increasingly dependent on government largesse, often care more about their personal security than about general freedom.

"Experience," wrote Justice Brandeis,

should teach us to be most on our guard to protect liberty when the government's purposes are beneficent. Men born to freedom are naturally alert to repel invasion of their liberty by evil-minded rulers. The greatest dangers to liberty lurk in insidious encroachments by men of zeal, well-meaning but without understanding.

The reason for this is that despotism appears in two distinct guises. There is the arbitrary rule of absolutist monarchs or dictators, elected by no one and subject neither to constitutional nor parliamentary restraints. And there is the tyranny in democratic societies of one part of the population over another: that of the majority over the minority but also—where elections are won with pluralities—of minorities over the majority.

Czarist Russia in its classical guise provided an extreme example of traditional despotism. There, the authorities could detain, imprison, or exile any subject without due process; they could confiscate his properties; they legislated as they saw fit. And yet, in practice, the average Russian under the old regime had scarcely any contact with the government and felt little interference from it, because the scope of government activity was very narrow, being largely confined to the collection or taxes, the drafting of recruits, and the preservation of the established order.

Today, the scope of government activity is immeasurably broader, and not only in authoritarian regimes but in a democracy like our own. Our government is elected, to be sure, but its interference in the life of citizens is greater than it has ever been. This is true at every level, from the federal down to that of the states and localities; in the latter, indeed, the recent expansion of government, partly under the aegis of "devolution," has reached striking proportions.

As Hayek pointed out, the broadening of the scope of government, in and of itself, carries seeds of a despotism at least as invidious as the traditional kind. Hayek's main concern was with protecting liberty from the seemingly unstoppable trend in Western democracies to subject the national economy to planning, which, he felt, would inevitably lead to tyranny. His fears in this respect proved unfounded. But his observations on the dangers implicit in the extension of the government's reach retain their validity:

[T]he probability of agreement of a substantial portion of the population upon a particular course of action decreases as the scope of state activity expands. . . . Democratic government worked successfully so long as, by a widely accepted creed, the functions of the state were limited to fields where real agreement among a majority could be achieved. The price we have to pay for a democratic system is the restriction of state action to those fields where agreement can be obtained; and it is the great merit of a liberal society that it reduces the necessity of agreement to a minimum compatible with the diversity of opinions which in a free society will exist.

This reasoning explains why government interference in the life of the citizenry even for benevolent purposes endangers liberty: it posits a consensus that does not exist and hence requires coercion.

But well-meaning patriarchalism also enervates people by robbing them of the entrepreneurial spirit implicit in freedom. What harm long-term dependence on the welfare state can inflict became apparent after the collapse of the Soviet Union, when a substantial part of the population, suddenly deprived of comprehensive state support and unaccustomed to fending for itself, came to yearn for the restoration of the despotic yoke.

To be sure, Soviet communism represented the most determined effort ever undertaken to condition people's thoughts and behavior, and nothing remotely like it is on the horizon in today's United States. Moreover, one can even point to a number of hopeful countervailing trends here, including recent decisions of the Supreme Court favoring property owners in their disputes with local authorities, the reform of welfare, and limitations on racial preferences in employment and higher education.

Nevertheless, for a variety of reasons, including the fact that our schools fail to teach history, the vast majority of today's citizens have no inkling to what they owe their liberty and prosperity—namely, a long and successful struggle for rights of which the right to property is the most fundamental. They are therefore unaware of what debilitating effect the restrictions on property rights will, over the long run, have on their lives.

The aristocrat Tocqueville, observing the democratic United States and his native bourgeois France a century and a half ago, had a premonition that the modern world faced dangers to liberty previously unknown. "I have no fear that they will meet with tyrants in their rulers," he wrote of future generations, "but rather with guardians." Such "guardians" would deprive people of liberty by gratifying their desires and would then exploit their dependence on such generosity. He foresaw a kind of democratic despotism in which "an innumerable multitude of men, all equal and alike," would incessantly strive to pursue "the petty and paltry pleasures with which they glut their lives." Hovering over them would be the benign paternalistic government—the modern welfare state:

For their happiness such a government willingly labors, but it chooses to be the sole and only arbiter of that happiness; it provides for their security, foresees and supplies their necessities, facilitates their pleasures, manages their principal concerns, directs their industry, regulates the descent of property, and subdivides their inheritances: what remains, but to spare them all the care of thinking and all the trouble of living?

Is this what we want?

Richard Pipes, Baird research professor of history at Harvard, is the author of numerous works, including *Russia Under the Regime, The Unknown Lenin,* and *The Russian Revolution.* The present essay appears in somewhat different form as the concluding chapter of his book, *Property and Freedom,* which will be published by Knopf.

Reading 24
WHY THERE IS A CULTURE WAR: GRAMSCI AND TOCQUEVILLE IN AMERICA
John Fonte

As intellectual historians have often had occasion to observe, there are times in a nation's history when certain ideas are just "in the air." Admittedly, this point seems to fizzle when applied to our *particular* historical moment. On the surface of American politics, as many have had cause to mention, it appears that the main trends predicted over a decade ago in Francis Fukuyama's "The End of History?" have come to pass—that ideological (if not partisan) strife has been muted; that there is a general consensus about the most important questions of the day (capitalism, not socialism; democracy, not authoritarianism); and that the contemporary controversies that do exist, while occasionally momentous, are essentially mundane, concerned with practical problem-solving (whether it is better to count ballots by hand or by machine) rather than with great principles.

And yet, I would argue, all that is true only on the surface. For simultaneously in the United States of the past few decades, recurring philosophical concepts have not only remained "in the air," but have proved influential, at times decisive, in cultural and legal and moral arguments about the most important questions facing the nation. Indeed: Prosaic appearances to the contrary, beneath the surface of American politics an intense ideological struggle is being waged between two competing worldviews. I will call these "Gramscian" and "Tocquevillian" after the intellectuals who authored the warring ideas: the twentieth-century Italian thinker Antonio Gramsci, and, of course, the nineteenth-century French intellectual Alexis de Tocqueville. The stakes in the battle between the intellectual heirs of these two men are no less than what kind of country the United States will be in decades to come.

REFINING CLASS WARFARE

We'll begin with an overview of the thought of Antonio Gramsci (1891–1937), a Marxist intellectual and politician. Despite his enormous influence on today's politics, he remains far less well-known to most Americans than does Tocqueville.

Gramsci's main legacy arises through his departures from orthodox Marxism. Like Marx, he argued that all societies in human history have been divided into two basic groups: the privileged and the marginalized, the oppressor and the oppressed, the dominant and the subordinate. Gramsci expanded Marx's ranks of the "oppressed" into categories that still endure. As he wrote in his famous *Prison Notebooks,* "The marginalized groups of history include not only the economically oppressed, but also women, racial minorities, and many 'criminals.'" What Marx and his orthodox followers described as "the people," Gramsci describes as an "ensemble" of subordinate groups and classes in every society that has ever existed until now. This collection of oppressed and marginalized groups, "the people," lack unity and, often, even consciousness of their own oppression. To reverse the correlation of power from the privileged to the "marginalized," then, was Gramsci's declared goal.

Power, in Gramsci's observation, is exercised by privileged groups or classes in two ways: through domination, force, or coercion; and through something called "hegemony," which means the ideological supremacy of a system of values that supports the class or group interests of the predominant classes or groups. Subordinate groups, he argued, are influenced to internalize the value systems and worldviews of the privileged groups and, thus, to consent to their own marginalization.

Far from being content with a mere uprising, therefore, Gramsci believed that it was necessary first to delegitimize the dominant belief systems of the predominant groups and to create a "counter-hegemony" (i.e., a new system of values for the subordinate groups) before the marginalized could be empowered. Moreover, because hegemonic values permeate all spheres of civil society—schools, churches, the media, voluntary associations—civil society itself, he argued, is the great battleground in the struggle for hegemony, the "war of position." From this point, too, followed a corollary for which Gramsci should be known (and which is echoed in the feminist slogan)—that *all* life is "political." Thus, private life, the workplace, religion, philosophy, art, and literature, and civil society, in general, are contested battlegrounds in the struggle to achieve societal transformation.

It is perhaps here that one sees Gramsci's most important reexamination of Marx's thought. Classical Marxists implied that a revolutionary consciousness would simply develop from the objective (and oppressive) material conditions of working class life. Gramsci disagreed, noting that "there have always been exploiters and exploited"—but very few *revolutions* per se. In his analysis, this was because subordinate groups usually lack the "clear theoretical consciousness" necessary to convert the "structure of repression into one of rebellion and social reconstruction." Revolutionary "consciousness" is crucial. Unfortunately, the subordinate groups possess "false consciousness," that is to say, they accept the conventional assumptions and values of the dominant groups, as "legitimate." But real change, he continued to believe, can only come about through the transformation of consciousness.

Just as Gramsci's analysis of consciousness is more nuanced than Marx's, so too is his understanding of the role of intellectuals in that process. Marx had argued that for revolutionary social transformation to be successful, the worldviews of the predominant groups must first be unmasked as instruments of domination. In classical Marxism, this crucial task of demystifying and delegitimizing the ideological hegemony of the dominant groups is performed by intellectuals. Gramsci, more subtly, distinguishes between two types of intellectuals: "traditional" and "organic." What subordinate groups need, Gramsci maintains, are their own "organic intellectuals." However, the defection of "traditional" intellectuals from the dominant groups to the subordinate groups, he held, is also important, because traditional intellectuals who have "changed sides" are well positioned within established institutions.

The metaphysics, or lack thereof, behind this Gramscian worldview are familiar enough. Gramsci describes his position as "absolute historicism," meaning that morals, values, truths, standards, and human nature itself are products of different historical epochs. There are no absolute moral standards that are universally true for all human beings outside of a particular historical context; rather, morality is "socially constructed."

Historically, Antonio Gramsci's thought shares features with other writers who are classified as "Hegelian Marxists"—the Hungarian Marxist Georg Lukacs, the German thinker Karl Korsch, and members of the "Frankfurt School" (e.g., Theodor Adomo and Herbert Marcuse), a group of theorists associated with the Institute for Social Research founded in Frankfurt, Germany in the 1920s, some of whom attempted to synthesize the thinking of Marx and Freud. All emphasized that the decisive struggle to overthrow the bourgeois regime (that is, middle-class liberal democracy) would be fought out at the level of consciousness. That is, the old order had to be rejected by its citizens intellectually and morally before any real transfer of power to the subordinate groups could be achieved.

GRAMSCI'S LONG REACH

The relation of all these abstractions to the nuts and bolts of American politics is, as the record shows, surprisingly direct. All of Gramsci's most innovative ideas—for example, that dominant and subordinate groups based on race, ethnicity, and gender are engaged in struggles over power; that the "personal is political"; and that all knowledge and morality are social constructions—are assumptions and presuppositions at the very center of today's politics. So too is the very core of the Gramscian-Hegelian worldview: group-based morality, or the idea that what is moral is what serves the interests of "oppressed" or "marginalized" ethnic, racial, and gender groups.[3]

What, for example, lies behind the concept of "jury nullification," a notion that now enjoys the support of law professors at leading universities? Building on the Hegelian-Marxist concepts of group power and group-based morality, jury nullification advocates argue that minorities serving on juries should use their "power" as jurors to refuse to convict minority defendants

regardless of the evidence presented in court, because the minority defendants have been "powerless," lifelong victims of an oppressive system that
is skewed in favor of dominant groups, such as white males.

Indeed, what is called "critical theory," a direct descendant of Gramscian
and Hegelian-Marxist thinking, is widely influential in both law and education. Critical legal studies posits that the law grows out of unequal relations
of power and therefore serves the interests of and legitimizes the rule of
dominant groups. Its subcategories include critical race theory and feminist
legal theory. The critical legal studies movement could hardly be more
Gramscian; it seeks to "deconstruct" bourgeois legal ideas that serve as
instruments of power for the dominant groups and "reconstruct" them to
serve the interests of the subordinate groups.

Or consider the echoes of Gramsci in the works of yet another law professor, Michigan's Catharine MacKinnon. She writes in *Toward a Feminist
Theory of the State* (1989), "The rule of law and the rule of men are one
thing, indivisible," because "State power, embodied in law, exists throughout
society as male power." Furthermore, "Male power is systemic. Coercive,
legitimated, and epistemic, it *is* the regime." Therefore, MacKinnon notes, "a
rape is not an isolated event or moral transgression or individual interchange
gone wrong but an act of terrorism and torture within a systemic context of
group subjection, like lynching." Similarly, MacKinnon has argued that sexual
harassment is essentially an issue of power exercised by the dominant over
the subordinate group.

Such thinking may begin in ivory towers, but it does not end there. The
United States Supreme Court adopted MacKinnon's theories as the basis for
its interpretation of sexual harassment law in the landmark *Meritor Savings
Bank v. Vinson* (1986). This is only one example of how major American
social policy has come to be based not on Judeo-Christian precepts nor on
Kantian-Enlightenment ethics, but on Gramscian and Hegelian-Marxist
concepts of group power.

HEGEL AMONG THE CEOS

Quite apart from their popularity among academics and in certain realms
of politics, Gramscian and Hegelian-Marxist ideas are also prominent in
three other major sectors of American civil society: foundations, universities,
and corporations. As laymen and analysts alike have observed over the
years, the major foundations—particularly Ford, Rockefeller, Carnegie, and
MacArthur—have for decades spent millions of dollars promoting "cutting
edge" projects on racial, ethnic, and gender issues. According to author and
foundation expert Heather MacDonald, for example, feminist projects received
$36 million from Ford, Rockefeller, Mellon, and other large foundations
between 1972 and 1992. Similarly, according to a Capital Research Center
report by Peter Warren, a policy analyst at the National Association of

Scholars, foundations have crowned diversity the "king" of American campuses. For example, the Ford Foundation launched a Campus Diversity Initiative in 1990 that funded programs in about 250 colleges and universities at a cost of approximately $15 million. The Ford initiative promotes what sounds like a Gramscian's group-rights dream: as Peter Warren puts it, "the establishment of racial, ethnic, and sex-specific programs and academic departments, group preferences in student admissions, group preferences in staff and faculty hiring, sensitivity training for students and staff, and campus-wide convocations to raise consciousness about the need for such programs."

Alan Kors, a history professor at the University of Pennsylvania, has described in detail how Ford and other foundation "diversity" grants are put to use. As he noted in "Thought Reform 101" in the March 2000 issue of *Reason,* "at almost all our campuses, some form of moral and political re-education has been built into freshman orientation." A "central goal of these programs," Kors states, "is to uproot 'internalized oppression,' a crucial concept in the diversity education planning documents of most universities." The concept of "internalized oppression" is the same as the Hegelian-Marxist notion of "false consciousness," in which people in the subordinate groups "internalize" (and thus accept) the values and ways of thinking of their oppressors in the dominant groups.

At Columbia University, for instance, new students are encouraged to get rid of "their own social and personal beliefs that foster inequality." To accomplish this, the assistant dean for freshmen, Katherine Balmer, insists that "training" is needed. At the end of freshman orientation at Bryn Mawr in the early 1990s, according to the school program, students were "breaking free" of "the cycle of oppression" and becoming "change agents." Syracuse University's multicultural program is designed to teach students that they live "in a world impacted by various oppression issues, including racism."

Kors states that at an academic conference sponsored by the University of Nebraska, the attendees articulated the view that "White students desperately need formal 'training' in racial and cultural awareness. The moral goal of such training should override white notions of privacy and individualism." One of the leading "diversity experts" providing scores of "training programs" in universities, corporations, and government bureaucracies is Hugh Vasquez of the Todos Institute of Oakland, California. Vasquez's study guide for a Ford Foundation-funded diversity film, *Skin Deep,* explains the meaning of "white privilege" and "internalized oppression" for the trainees. It also explains the concept of an "ally," as an individual from the "dominant group" who rejects his "unmerited privilege" and becomes an advocate for the position of the subordinate groups. This concept of the "ally," of course, is Gramscian to the core; it is exactly representative of the notion that subordinate groups struggling for power must try to "conquer ideologically" the traditional intellectuals or activist cadres normally associated with the dominant group.

The employees of America's major corporations take many of the same sensitivity training programs as America's college students, often from the same "diversity facilitators." Frederick Lynch, the author of the *Diversity Machine*, reported "diversity training" is rampant among the Fortune 500. Even more significant, on issues of group preferences vs. individual opportunity, major corporate leaders tend to put their money and influence behind group rights instead of individual rights.

After California voters passed Proposition 209, for example—a referendum outlawing racial and gender preferences in employment—Ward Connerly, the African-American businessman who led the effort, launched a similar antipreferences initiative in the state of Washington. The Washington initiative, I-200, read as follows: "The State shall not discriminate against or grant preferential treatment to, any individual or group on the basis of race, sex, color, ethnicity, or national origin in the operation of public employment, or public contracting." This language was almost identical to California's Proposition 209. *Atlantic Monthly* editor Michael Kelly reported in *The Washington Post* on August 23 that when asked his opinion on Proposition 209 during the referendum debate, Sen. Joseph Lieberman replied, "I can't see how I could be opposed to it . . . It is basically a statement of American values . . . and says we shouldn't discriminate in favor of somebody based on the group they represent."

However, Washington's *business* leaders disagreed. In his autobiography *Creating Equal,* Ward Connerly wrote that the "most important significant obstacle we faced in Washington was not the media, or even political personalities, but the corporate world . . . Boeing, Weyerhauser, Starbucks, Costco, and Eddie Bauer all made huge donations to the No on I-200 campaign . . . The fundraising was spearheaded by Bill Gates, Sr., a regent of the University of Washington, whose famous name seemed to suggest that the whole of the high-tech world was solemnly shaking its head at us."

Interestingly, private corporations are also more supportive of another form of group rights—gay rights—than are government agencies at any level. As of June 2000, for example, approximately 100 Fortune 500 companies had adopted health benefits for same-sex partners. According to the gay rights organization, Human Rights Campaign, the companies offering same-sex benefits include the leading corporations in the Fortune 500 ranking: among the top 10, General Motors (ranked first), Ford (fourth), IBM (sixth), AT&T (eighth), and Boeing (tenth), as well as Hewlett-Packard, Merrill Lynch, Chase Manhattan Bank, Bell Atlantic, Chevron, Motorola, Prudential, Walt Disney, Microsoft, Xerox, and United Airlines. Corporate reaction to gay activist attacks on Dr. Laura Schlessinger is another indication of how Hegelian-Gramscian the country's business leaders have become. Sears and EchoStar have lately joined a long list of advertisers— Procter and Gamble, Xerox, AT&T, Toys R Us, Kraft, General Foods, and Geico—in pulling their advertising from the popular talk show host.

Whether these decisions favoring gay (read: group) rights were motivated by ideology, economic calculation, or an opportunistic attempt to appear "progressive," they typify American businesses' response to the culture war.

THE TOCQUEVILLIAN COUNTERATTACK

The primary resistance to the advance of Gramscian ideas comes from an opposing quarter that I will call contemporary Tocquevillianism. Its representatives take Alexis de Tocqueville's essentially empirical description of American exceptionalism and celebrate the traits of this exceptionalism as normative values to be embraced. As Tocqueville noted in the 1830s (and as the World Values Survey, a scholarly comparative assessment, reaffirmed in the 1990s), Americans are different from Europeans in several crucial respects. Two recent books—Seymour Martin Lipset's *American Exceptionalism* (1997) and Michael Ledeen's *Tocqueville on American Character* (2000)— have made much the same point: that Americans today, just as in Tocqueville's time, are much more individualistic, religious, and patriotic than the people of any other comparably advanced nation.[4]

What was particularly exceptional for Tocqueville (and contemporary Tocquevillians) is the singular American path to modernity. Unlike other modernists, Americans combined strong religious and patriotic beliefs with dynamic, restless entrepreneurial energy that emphasized equality of individual opportunity and eschewed hierarchical and ascriptive group affiliations. The trinity of American exceptionalism could be described as (1) dynamism (support for equality of individual opportunity, entrepreneurship, and economic progress); (2) religiosity (emphasis on character development, mores, and voluntary cultural associations) that works to contain the excessive individual egoism that dynamism sometimes fosters; and (3) patriotism (love of country, self-government, and support for constitutional limits).

Among today's Tocquevillians we could include—public intellectuals William Bennett, Michael Novak, Gertrude Himrnelfarb, Marvin Olasky, Norman Podhoretz, and former Clinton White House advisor and political philosopher William Galston, and scholars Wilfred McClay, Harvey Mansfield, and Walter MacDougall. Neoconservatives, traditional conservatives of the *National Review*-Heritage Foundation stripe, some students of political philosopher Leo Strauss, and some centrist Democrats are Tocquevillian in their emphasis on America's special path to modernity that combines aspects of the pre-modern (emphasis on religion, objective truth, and transcendence) with the modern (self-government, constitutional liberalism, entrepreneurial enterprise). The writings of neoconservative Irving Kristol and *National Review*-style conservative Charles Kesler clarify this special American path to modernity. Like thoughtful scholars before them, both make a sharp distinction between the moderate (and positive)

Enlightenment (of Locke, Montesquieu, and Adam Smith) that gave birth to the American Revolution and the radical (and negative) Enlightenment (Condorcet and the *philosophes*) that gave birth to the Revolution in France.

Like their ideological opposites, Tocquevillians are also represented in business and government. In the foundation world, prevailing Gramscian ideas have been challenged by scholars funded by the Bradley, Olin, and Scaife foundations. For example, Michael Joyce of Bradley has called his foundation's approach "Tocquevillian" and supported associations and individuals that foster moral and religious underpinnings to self-help and civic action. At the same time, Joyce called in "On Self-Government" (*Policy Review,* July–August 1998) for challenging the "political hegemony" of the service providers and "scientific managers" who run the "therapeutic state" that Tocqueville feared would result in "an immense and tutelary" power that threatened liberty. As for the political world, a brief list of those influenced by the Tocquevillian side of the argument would include, for example, Sen. Daniel Coats of Indiana, Sen. Joseph Lieberman of Connecticut, and Gov. George W. Bush of Texas. All have supported Tocquevillian initiatives and employed Tocquevillian language in endorsing education and welfare measures that emphasize the positive contributions of faith and responsibility.

There is also a third category to be considered here: those institutions and individuals that also oppose the Gramscian challenge, but who are not Tocquevillians because they reject one or more features of the trinity of American exceptionalism. For example, *Reason* magazine editor Virginia Postrel sees the world divided into pro-change "dynamists" and anti-change "statists." Postrel's libertarianism emphasizes only one aspect of American exceptionalism, its dynamism, and slights the religious and patriotic pillars that in the Tocquevillian synthesis provide the nation's moral and civic core.

Similarly, paleoconservatives such as Samuel Francis, a leading Buchananite intellectual, oppose modernism and the Enlightenment in all its aspects, not simply its radical wing. Likewise secular patriots such as historian Arthur Schlesinger Jr. embrace a positive form of enlightened American nationalism, but are uncomfortable with the religious and entrepreneurial (including the antistatist) traditions that complete the Tocquevillian trinity. Catholic social democrats like E. J. Dionne accept the religious part of the Tocquevillian trinity, but would like to curb its risky dynamism and deemphasize its patriotism.

A few years ago, several conservative and religious intellectuals writing in a *First Things* magazine symposium suggested that American liberal democracy was facing a crisis of legitimacy. One of the symposium writers, Judge Robert Bork, suggests in his book *Slouching Towards Gomorrah* that "revolutionary" upheavals of the 1960s were "not a complete break with the spirit of the American past," but inherent in the Enlightenment framework of America's founding principles. Bork and others—including Paul Weyrich and Cal Thomas—appear to have speculated that perhaps America's path to modernity was itself flawed (too much dynamism and too little morality). What could be called a partial Tocquevillian position of some conservative intellectuals and activists could be contrasted with the work of American Catholic Whigs—for example, the American Enterprise Institute's Michael Novak and the Faith and Reason Institute's Robert Royal—who have argued, in essence, that America's founding principles are sound and that the three elements of the Tocquevillian synthesis (entrepreneurial dynamism, religion, and patriotism) are at the heart of the American experience and of America's exceptional contribution to the idea of ordered liberty.

At the end of the day it is unlikely that the libertarians, paleoconservatives, secular patriots, Catholic social democrats, or disaffected religious right intellectuals will mount an effective resistance to the continuing Gramscian assault. Only the Tocquevillians appear to have the strength—in terms of intellectual firepower, infrastructure, funding, media attention, and a comprehensive philosophy that taps into core American principles—to challenge the Gramscians with any chance of success.

TOCQUEVILLIANISM AS PRAXIS

Writing in *Policy Review* in 1996, Adam Meyerson described the task of cultural renewal as "applied Tocquevillianism." In explaining one of his key points, Tocqueville writes in *Democracy in America* that "mores" are central to the "Maintenance of a Democratic Republic in the United States." He defines "mores" as not only "the habits of the heart," but also the "different notions possessed by men, the various opinions current among them, and the sum of ideas that shape mental habits"—in short, he declares, "the whole moral and intellectual state of a people."

One of the leading manifestos of the Tocquevillians is "A Call to Civil Society: Why Democracy Needs Moral Truths," published by the Council on Civil Society. It outlines the traditional civic and moral values (Tocqueville's "mores") that buttress the republic. The document (endorsed by, among others, Sens. Coats and Lieberman, in addition to Don Eberly, Jean Bethke Elshtain, Francis Fukuyama, William Galston, Glenn Loury, Cornel West, James Q. Wilson, and Daniel Yankelovitch) states that the "civic truths" of the American regime are "those of Western constitutionalism, rooted in both classical understandings of natural law and natural right and in the Judeo-Christian religious tradition. . . . The moral truths that make possible our experiment in self-government," according to this statement, "are in large part biblical and religious," informed by the "classical natural law tradition" and the "ideas of the Enlightenment." The "most eloquent expressions" of these truths are "found in the Declaration of Independence, Washington's

Farewell Address, Lincoln's Gettysburg Address and Second Inaugural Address, and King's Letter from the Birmingham Jail."

The Tocquevillians, then, emphasize "renewing" and "rediscovering" American mores, suggesting that there is a healthy civic and moral core to the American regime that needs to be brought back to life. Moreover, if the first task is cultural renewal, the second task is cultural transmission. Thus, the "Call to Civil Society" declares that the "central task of every generation is moral transmission." Religion, in particular, "has probably been the primary force" that "transmits from one generation to another the moral understandings that are essential to liberal democratic institutions," Moreover, "[at] their best . . . our houses of worship foster values that are essential to human flourishing and democratic civil society, personal responsibility, respect for moral law, and neighbor-love or concern for others." In addition, the statement declares that a "basic responsibility of the school is cultural transmission," particularly "a knowledge of [the] country's constitutional heritage, an understanding of what constitutes good citizenship, and an appreciation of [this] society's common civic faith and shared moral philosophy."

In the matter of practice, the past few years have also witnessed what could be called "Tocquevillian" initiatives that attempt to bring faith-based institutions (particularly churches) into federal and state legislative efforts to combat welfare and poverty. In the mid-1990s, Sen. Coats, working with William Bennett and other intellectuals, introduced a group of 19 bills known as the Project for American Renewal. Among other things these bills advocated dollar for dollar tax credits for contributions to charitable organizations, including churches. Coats's goal in introducing this legislation was to push the debate in a Tocquevillian direction, by getting policy makers thinking about new ways of involving religious and other civic associations in social welfare issues. Coats and others were asking why the faith community was being excluded from participating in federal social programs. At the same time there are other Tocquevillians, including Michael Horowitz of the Hudson Institute, who favor tax credits, but worry that by accepting federal grant money the faith institutions could become dependent on government money and adjust their charitable projects to government initiatives.

In 1996 Congress included a "charitable choice" provision in the landmark welfare reform legislation. The charitable choice section means that if a state receives federal funds to provide services, it could not discriminate against religious organizations if they wanted to compete for federal grants to provide those services. The section includes guidelines designed simultaneously to protect both the religious character of the faith-based institutions receiving the federal funds and the civil rights of the individuals using the services. However, in 1998 the Clinton administration attempted to dilute the "charitable choice" concept in another piece of legislation by stating that administration lawyers opposed giving funds to what they described as "pervasively sectarian" institutions that could be inferred to mean churches doing charitable work.

Besides activity at the federal level, some states have started similar projects. Faithworks Indiana, a center sponsored by the state government, assists faith-based institutions with networking. In Illinois, state agencies are reaching out to faith-based institutions through the "Partners for Hope" program. In Mississippi Governor Kirk Fordice launched the "Faith and Families" program with the ambitious goal of linking each of the state's 5,000 churches with a welfare recipient.

Both Gov. George W. Bush in Texas and Sen. Joseph Lieberman in Congress have been friendly to some Tocquevillian approaches to legislation. Bush has promoted legislation to remove licensing barriers to church participation in social programs. He has also supported faith initiatives in welfare-to-work and prison reform projects. Lieberman supported the charitable choice provision of the welfare reform act and co-sponsored the National Youth Crime Prevention Demonstration Act that would promote "violence free zones" by working with grass-roots organizations, including faith-based organizations.

LEGISLATIVE BATTLEGROUNDS

Gramscian concepts have been on the march through Congress in recent years, meeting in at least some cases Tocquevillian resistance and counterattack. For example, the intellectual underpinning for the Gender Equity in Education Act of 1993 (and most gender equity legislation going back to the seminal Women's Educational Equity Act, or WEEA, of the 1970s) is the essentially Gramscian and Hegelian-Marxist concept of "systemic" or "institutionalized oppression." In this view, the mainstream institutions of society, including the schools, enforce an "oppressive" system (in this case, a "patriarchy") at the expense of a subordinate group (i.e., women and girls).

The work of Harvard education professor Carol Gilligan, promoted by the American Association of University Women (AAUW), was influential in persuading Congress to support the Gender Equity in Education Act. Professor Gilligan identifies the main obstacles to educational opportunity for American girls as the "patriarchial social order," "androcentric and patriarchical norms," and "Western thinking"—that is to say, the American "system" itself is at fault.

In speaking on behalf of the bill, Republican Senator Olympia Snowe of Maine made a Gramscian case, decrying "systemic discrimination against girls." Democratic Rep. Patsy Mink of Hawaii likewise attacked the "pervasive nature" of anti-female bias in the educational system. Maryland Republican Rep. Connie Morella declared that throughout the schools "inequitable practices are widespread and persistent." Nor surprisingly, she insisted that "gender equity training" for "teachers, counselors, and administrators" be made available with federal funds. As noted earlier, one of the remedies to "systemic oppression" is "training" (of the "reeducation" type described by Professor Kors) that seeks to alter the "consciousness" of individuals in both the dominant groups and subordinate groups. Thus, Sen. Snowe also advocated "training" programs to eliminate "sexual harassment in its very early stages in our Nation's schools."

In a related exercise in Gramscian reasoning, Congress in 1994 passed the Violence Against Women Act. According to Democratic Senator Joseph Biden of Delaware, the "whole purpose" of the bill was "to raise the consciousness of the American public." The bill's supporters charged that there was an "epidemic" of violent crime against women. Echoing Catharine MacKinnon (e.g., rape is "not an individual act" but "terrorism" within a "systemic context of group subjection like lynching"), the bill's proponents filled the *Congressional Record* with the group-based (and Hegelian-Marxist) concept that women were being attacked because they were women and belonged to a subordinate group. It was argued by bill's proponents that these "violent attacks" are a form of "sex discrimination," "motivated by gender," and that they "reinforce and maintain the disadvantaged status of women as a group." Moreover, the individual attacks create a "climate of fear that makes all women afraid to step out of line." Although there was no serious social science evidence of an "epidemic" of violence against women, the almost Marxist-style agitprop campaign worked, and the bill passed.

In 1991, the Congress passed a civil rights bill that altered a Supreme Court decision restricting racial and gender group remedies. The new bill strengthened the concept of "disparate impact," which is a group-based notion that employment practices are discriminatory if they result in fewer members of "protected classes" (minorities and women) being hired than their percentage of the local workforce would presumably warrant.

Nine years later, in June 2000, the U.S. Senate passed the Hate Crimes Prevention Act, which would expand the category of hate crimes to include crimes motivated by hatred of women, gays, and the disabled (such crimes would receive stiffer sentences than crimes that were not motivated by hatred based on gender, sexual orientation, or disability status). In supporting the bill, Republican Sen. Gordon Smith of Oregon declared, "I have come to realize that hate crimes are different" because although they are "visited upon one person" they "are really directed at an entire community" (for example, the disabled community or the gay community). Democratic Sen. John Kerry of Massachusetts supported the legislation because, he insisted, "Standing law has proven inadequate in the protection of many victimized groups."

In a *Wall Street Journal* opinion piece, Dorothy Rabinowitz penned a Tocquevillian objection to this Gramscian legislation. Rabinowitz argued that hate crimes legislation undermined the traditional notion of equality under the law by "promulgating the fantastic argument that one act of violence is more significant than another because of the feelings that motivated the criminal." Using egalitarian and antihierarchical (that is, Tocquevillian) rhetoric, Rabinowitz declared that Americans "don't require two sets of laws: one for crimes against government-designated victims, the other for the rest of America."

THE SUPREME COURT AND THE WHITE HOUSE

Like the Congress, the Supreme Court has witnessed intense arguments over core political principles recognizable as Gramscian and Tocquevillian. Indeed, the court itself often serves as a near-perfect microcosm of the clash between these opposing ideas.

A provision of the Violence Against Women Act, for example, that permitted women to sue their attackers in federal rather than state courts was overturned by a deeply divided Supreme Court 5-4. The majority argued on federalist grounds that states had primacy in this criminal justice area. In another 5-4 decision the Supreme Court in 1999 ruled that local schools are subject to sexual discrimination suits under Title IX if their administrators fail to stop sexual harassment among schoolchildren. The case, *Davis v. Monroe County Board of Education,* involved two 10-year-olds in the fifth grade. Justice Anthony Kennedy broke tradition by reading a stinging dissent from the bench. He was joined by Justices Rehnquist, Scalia, and Thomas. Justice Kennedy attacked the majority view that the actions by the 10-year-old boy constituted "gender discrimination."

American Enterprise Institute scholar Christina Hoff Sommers in *The War Against Boys* noted that the court majority appears to accept the position of gender feminist groups that sexual harassment is "a kind of hate crime used by men to maintain and enforce the inferior status of women." Thus, Sommers explains, in terms of feminist theory (implicitly accepted by the court), the 10-year-old boy "did not merely upset and frighten" the ten-year-old girl, "he demeaned her as a member of a socially subordinate group." In effect, the court majority in *Davis* endorsed Gramscian and Hegelian-Marxist assumptions of power relations between dominant and subordinate groups and applied those assumptions to American fifth graders.

Recently, a similarly divided Supreme Court has offered divergent rulings on homosexual rights. In June 2000 the court overturned the New Jersey State Supreme Court and ruled 5-4 in *Boy Scouts of America v. Dale* that the Boy Scouts did not have to employ an openly gay scoutmaster. The majority's reasoning was quintessentially Tocquevillian—the First Amendment right of "freedom of association." Writing for the majority, Chief Justice Rehnquist declared that "judicial disapproval" of a private organization's values "does not justify the state's effort to compel the organization to accept members where such acceptance" would change the

organization's message. The law, Rehnquist continued, "is not free to interfere with speech for no better reason than promoting an approved message
or discouraging a disfavored one, however enlightened either purpose may
strike the government."

The dissent written by Justice Stevens, by contrast, declared that the states
have the "right" to social experimentation. Stevens noted that "atavistic
opinions" about women, minorities, gays, and aliens were the result of "traditional ways of thinking about members of unfamiliar classes." Moreover,
he insisted, "such prejudices are still prevalent" and "have caused serious
and tangible harm to members of the class (gays) New Jersey seeks to protect." Thus, the dissenters in this case agreed with the New Jersey Supreme
Court that the state had "a compelling interest in eliminating the destructive
consequences of discrimination from society" by requiring the Boy Scouts to
employ gay scoutmasters.

In 1992 Colorado voters in a referendum adopted Amendment 2 to the state
constitution barring local governments and the state from adding "homosexual orientation" as a specific category in city and state anti-discrimination
ordinances. In 1996 in *Romer v. Evans,* the U.S. Supreme Court in a 6-3 ruling
struck down Colorado's Amendment 2. The court majority rejected the state
of Colorado's position that the amendment "does no more than deny homosexuals special rights." The amendment, the court declared, "imposes a
broad disability" on gays, "nullifies specific legal protections for this class
(gays)," and infers "animosity towards the class that it affects." Further, the
majority insists that Amendment 2, "in making a general announcement that
gays and lesbians shall not have any particular protections from the law,
inflicts on them immediate, continuing, and real injuries."

Justice Anton Scalia wrote a blistering dissent that went straight to the
Gramscian roots of the decision. He attacked the majority "for inventing a
novel and extravagant constitutional doctrine to take victory away from the
traditional forces," and for "verbally disparaging as bigotry adherence to
traditional attitudes." "The court," Scalia wrote, "takes sides in the culture
war"; it "sides with the knights," that is, the elites, "reflecting the views and
values of the lawyer class." He concluded that: "Amendment 2 is designed
to prevent the piecemeal deterioration of the sexual morality favored by the
majority of Coloradans, and is not only an appropriate means to that legitimate end, but a means that Americans have employed before. Striking it
down is an act, not of judicial judgment, but of political will."

Finally, Gramscian and Hegelian-Marxist concepts have advanced in the
executive branch as well. In the 1990s, the federal government attempted both
to limit speech that adversely effected subordinate groups and to promote
group-based equality of result instead of equality of individual opportunity.

In 1994, for example, three residents of Berkeley, California protested
a federal Department of Housing and Urban Development (HUD) plan to build
subsidized housing for the homeless and mentally ill in their neighborhood.

The residents wrote protest letters and organized their neighbors. HUD officials investigated the Berkeley residents for "discrimination" against the disabled and threatened them with $100,000 in fines. The government offered to drop their investigation (and the fines) if the neighborhood residents promised to stop speaking against the federal housing project.

Heather MacDonald reported in *The Wall Street Journal* that one lawyer supporting HUD's position argued that if the Berkeley residents' protest letters resulted in the "denial of housing to a protected class of people, it ceases to be protected speech and becomes proscribed conduct." This is classic Hegelian-Marxist thinking—actions (including free speech) that "objectively" harm people in a subordinate class are unjust (and should be outlawed). Eventually, HUD withdrew its investigation. Nevertheless, the Berkeley residents brought suit against the HUD officials and won.

In 1999, to take another example, *The Wall Street Journal* reported that for the first time in American history the federal government was planning to require all companies doing business with the government to give federal officials the name, age, sex, race, and salary of every employee in the company during routine affirmative action audits. The purpose of the new plan, according to Secretary of Labor Alexis Herman, was to look for "racial and gender pay disparities." The implicit assumption behind the Labor Department's action is that "pay disparities" as such constitute a problem that requires a solution, even if salary differences are not the result of intentional discrimination. The Labor Department has long suggested that the continued existence of these disparities is evidence of "institutionalized discrimination."

TRANSMISSION—OR TRANSFORMATION

The slow but steady advance of Gramscian and Hegelian-Marxist ideas through the major institutions of American democracy, including the Congress, courts, and executive branch, suggests that there are two different levels of political activity in twenty-first century America. On the surface, politicians seem increasingly inclined to converge on the center. Beneath, however, lies a deeper conflict that is ideological in the most profound sense of the term and that will surely continue in decades to come, regardless of who becomes president tomorrow, or four or eight or even 20 years from now.

As we have seen, Tocquevillians and Gramscians clash on almost everything that matters. Tocquevillians believe that there are objective moral truths applicable to all people at all times. Gramscians believe that moral "truths" are subjective and depend upon historical circumstances. Tocquevillans believe that these civic and moral truths must be revitalized in order to remoralize society. Gramscians believe that civic and moral "truths" must be socially constructed by subordinate groups in order to achieve political and cultural liberation. Tocquevillians believe that functionaries like teachers and police officers represent legitimate authority.

Gramscians believe that teachers and police officers "objectively" represent power, not legitimacy. Tocquevillians believe in personal responsibility. Gramscians believe that "the personal is political." In the final analysis, Tocquevillians favor the *transmission* of the American regime; Gramscians, its *transformation*.

While economic Marxism appears to be dead, the Hegelian variety artic-ulated by Gramsci and others has not only survived the fall of the Berlin Wall, but also gone on to challenge the American republic at the level of its most cherished ideas. For more than two centuries America has been an "exceptional" nation, one whose restless entrepreneurial dynamism has been tempered by patriotism and a strong religious-cultural core. The ultimate triumph of Gramscianism would mean the end of this very "exceptionalism." America would at last become Europeanized: statist, thoroughly secular, post-patriotic, and concerned with group hierarchies and group rights in which the idea of equality before the law as traditionally understood by Americans would finally be abndoned. Beneath the surface of our seemingly placid times, the ideological, political, and historical stakes are enormous.

John Fonte is a senior fellow at the Hudson Institute.

Reading 25
WHY THE MIDDLE CLASS IS THE KEY TO WINNING THE POLITICAL CORRECTNESS WAR
George Zilbergeld

> In this country, the coming of the post-industrial age may mean the loss of all that made America new—the only new thing in the world. America will no longer be the common man's continent. The common people of Europe eloped with history to America and lived in common-law marriage with it, unhallowed by the incantations of men of words. But the elites are finally catching up with us. We can hear the swish of leather as saddles are heaved on our backs. The intellectuals and the young, booted and spurred, feel themselves born to ride us.
> *Eric Hoffer*—First Things, Last Things

One cannot be part of a college or university today without recognizing the existence and increasing dominance of a group of professors and adminis-trators who are intensely hostile toward Western civilization, the United States, and white males. Unfortunately, most people have neither the time nor the inclination to devote much time to thinking about the odious legacy of political correctness. Unlike the "intelligentsia," most people, as Joseph Schumpeter noted, have jobs that do not concentrate on the spoken and written word and have direct responsibility for practical affairs.[5]

Non-intellectuals may dislike political correctness because they feel it stifles freedom of expression, and they may have the impression that its more fervent supporters are cranks. Yet they have a hard time plumbing the ideological depths of this movement, let alone understanding why they should be angry and demand an end to it.

Engaging non-intellectuals is necessary for turning the tide. As long as this battle is viewed primarily as between two groups of intellectuals, the politically correct will continue to win it, since they dominate both academe and the popular media.

Because the politically correct seek to reduce the political power and personal liberty of the common person, the basic strategy for engaging common people in this issue should be to show that it is in their self-interest to oppose PC. It is necessary to point out that almost any member of the middle class who is not also a member of a government-preferred minority group is automatically an object of PC scorn and derision. In short, the best way to convince people that their future depends on a successful fight against PC is to make clear to them that they are among the groups the politically correct love to hate.

Hatred is prominent in PC thought and thus affords the best view into the collective soul of this movement. Whether the topic is AIDS, the role of punishment in reducing criminality, welfare, or environmentalism, the politically correct oppose the rights of the wider society in order to increase their own special position and power.

Political correctness sees the world as a place of absolute good and evil, with Western civilization, the United States, white males, and capitalism as the basic forces of evil. According to this view, the key to a better world is to eliminate or weaken these forces. Although the politically correct speak often of empowerment, their goal is to *reduce* the power of most of the population while enhancing their own power. Most proponents of PC have jobs dealing primarily with words, without direct responsibility for practical affairs.[6]

The politically correct movement toward some form of socialism, or at least greater government control of the economy, tangibly reduces individual freedom. What must be made clear to non-intellectuals is that this hatred of capitalism is not peculiar to academic Marxist cranks. Rather, it is embedded in the rules and regulations created and enforced by the federal bureaucracy and inhibits the ability of people to run businesses and to buy products most efficiently. PC hostility to individual autonomy in the marketplace impinges directly on the average consumer.

In foreign affairs, the politically correct nearly always sympathize with enemies of the United States. Thus, if it is a choice between the United States and North Vietnam, they side with North Vietnam. Note the intensity in their voices when the politically correct condemn the United States for global "insensitivity," and the gentle condemnation, if any, with which they address communist atrocities. Note, too, the loving attention to detail

with which they discuss the sins of the United States and the vague gener-
alities they employ and forgetfulness they seem to acquire when discussing
communist regimes. Lenin was correct to call such misguided apologists
"useful idiots."

The politically correct's disdain for democracy is obvious in their unwill-
ingness to trust voters to implement or support sound policies. Instead, they
rely on the least democratic institutions: judges and bureaucrats. It is now
commonplace to see important policy decisions in such areas as group preferences, busing, the death penalty, and, most important, the educational
system, made not by "the people," but by political appointees.

Unfortunately, the media focus only on the more bizarre and extreme
examples of political correctness. When only these examples are publicized,
the public may regard the politically correct as merely eccentric, rather than
as a real and immediate threat to our way of life.

The fear of empowering individuals to understand the world on their
own can be seen in PC education. This issue, more than any other, ought to
be used to arrest the attention of those uninterested in the debate. Even
political cynics care about the education of their children. Most people care
about whether their children are learning the skills they will need for a prosperous career or being fed politically correct propaganda. An emphasis on
practical issues such as education will help win the culture war.

If the politically correct cannot condemn the West outright, then they
seek to reduce its importance by claiming that all civilizations and cultures
are equal—the so-called "moral equivalence" doctrine. This effectively
reduces the worth of Western values, notably individual liberty.

Many Americans have probably concluded that most college professors
are cranks to be forgotten shortly after graduation, and thus are not much
concerned with the PC domination of academe. But when they understand
that the politically correct intend to dominate far more than speech on
campus—the public debate on such issues as sex education, where children
go to school, how middle-class values are portrayed in school, how the
United States military is portrayed, and how criminals are punished—they
will enter the fray.

Those with the most to lose from the PC are the middle class, which in the
view of the politically correct has one great sin: it runs its own affairs and does
not have a great need for government services or special legal status. True,
when people in the middle class are old, sick, or want an education, they often
call on the government, but they do not need a self-anointed politically correct
elite to protect their interests. The middle class runs itself, and it cannot be
used as a front for gaining power, as can the poor and minorities.

As Eric Hoffer noted:

The middle class is the least elitist ruling class we know of. Not only is it wide
open to all comers, but it aspires to a state of affairs in which things happen of

themselves . . . Unlike any other ruling classes, the middle class has found it convenient to operate on the assumption that if you leave people alone they will perform tolerably well; and under no other ruling class have common people shown such willingness to exert themselves to the utmost. It is the fabulously productive, more or less self-regulating chaos of a society that has given the modern age its singular spirit and set it off from all preceding centuries. Regimentation and minute regulation are as ancient as civilization. Small wonder that elitists of every stripe . . . have viewed middle class society . . . as an abomination.[7]

The middle class is one of the few groups that can be attacked without fear of retaliation, and it is the group that will pay the highest price for harmful politically correct programs. For example, the New Jersey Supreme Court has demanded that the state provide as much money for the poorest school districts as is spent in the richest ones. The result is that middle class New Jersey residents are now forced to pay more to educate other peoples' children than for their own. This, despite the New Jersey Supreme Court admitting it has no evidence that money is the key factor in a quality education. It is the middle class whose children will be bused; it is the middle class who will be taxed to support PC social engineering; it is the middle class child who will be kept out of an elite college because he or she is not of a "preferred" racial, ethnic, or economic group.

The categories of race, class, and gender are ways of imprisoning the individual in biological or abstract cultural types. For instance, in PC America a black person is expected to have particular characteristics and to take certain political positions that mimic those of the politically correct elite (e.g., hatred of capitalism and a generalized disdain for American society). Whether the group is a race, a class, or a gender, the chosen favorites of the politically correct are expected to condemn those the politically correct condemn and attack those the politically correct attack. Otherwise, the people in the favored groups are not considered truly representative of their groups. Note the incredible spectacle of the politically correct stating that some people with dark skin are not racially "authentic." Ideological position and not skin color dominates politically correct race talk.

Why do the politically correct support providing benefits to those who claim a special victim status, and often prefer the less qualified members of society to the more qualified? Any admissions officer can admit the hard working middle-class child to a college; it is when he admits the "street person," runaway, or criminal that he shows his superior compassion for and "sensitivity" toward others. Why do the politically correct choose to sympathize with criminals, and not their victims? Again, it is a chance to show that they see what others less wise do not see.

Much leftist thought, especially political correctness, revolves around the idea of secret or special sources of knowledge. Thus, to use the Marxist paradigm, while others only see the "substructure" of society (the material conditions of everyday life), the politically correct see the "super-structure," the ideological complex that common folk reify and treat as concrete entities of existence. While the ordinary person sees only what *appears* to be the cause of crime (i.e., the criminal), leftist intellectuals see the real, "underlying" causes of crime,[8] which generally involve "power differentials," "class antagonisms," "the awakening of a nascent class consciousness," "low self-esteem," "institutionalized racism," and on and on, *ad nauseam*.

Is human nature infinitely plastic? If it is, then the politically correct are needed to mold that nature. Is it necessary to acquire a special vocabulary to talk about society? If it is, then the politically correct are needed to teach that vocabulary. Is there a need to understand the "underlying" causes of crime? If there is, then surely it is necessary to acknowledge the superiority of those who possess this special knowledge and to listen to their analysis of what society should do to alleviate the evil conditions that prevail.

Unfortunately for the politically correct, most Americans support the death penalty, oppose busing to achieve racial balance, and think welfare recipients should be required to work. Most Americans believe in individual responsibility and that reward should depend on effort. Most Americans think it is natural, reasonable, and good to care more about one's family than about strangers, more about one's countrymen than about foreigners, and about the death of one's country's soldiers. The PC are thus badly out-numbered by potential enemies.

We must emphasize to those we are trying to win to our side that the heart of the matter is the empowerment of the individual to make his own choices and to make his own way in the world. This fight is as old as human history—the fight between those who support liberty and those who believe that their special knowledge and vision gives them the right to coerce others.

The strategy for defeating the politically correct entails pointing out to the average person the threat the PC poses to him. Once people are convinced that they will lose something substantial, they will become interested and join the battle. The fight must be sold as a series of benefits that the politically correct would deny to the average member of the middle class. The other aspect of this strategy entails building a sense of confidence that the battle is winnable. This can be achieved by pointing out that most of the liberal intellectuals live off of the middle class. Most politically correct professors—who have not been off a college campus since they slept at home, and who could not earn a living outside academe—are totally dependent on the working people they despise. We are probably faced with the world's largest "the emperor has no clothes" situation. Once the middle class recognizes this, and combines this insight with awareness of the damage done to them, the battle is won.

Reading 26
THE "BANALITY OF EVIL" AND THE POLITICAL
CULTURE OF HATRED
Paul Hollander

There was a time when the most massive and premeditated forms of political violence, exemplified by the Holocaust were associated with the "banality of evil"—a concept introduced by Hannah Arendt. She popularized the idea that the Holocaust was a form of bureaucratized mass murder carried out by "desk murderers" who had no strong feelings about it, perfectly ordinary human beings, such as Eichman and his associates, impersonal and interchangeable cogs in the gigantic killing machine. Anybody could have performed the task; no political passion or ideological conviction was involved or required. It was implied that this type of violence was emblematic of modernity and mass society and their key characteristics: anonymity, standardization, homogenization, impersonality as well as increasing specialization and reliance on technology. Stanley Milgram's experiments on obedience to authority further bolstered the notion that people are able and willing to inflict great pain and suffering on total strangers for no reason other than their willingness to obey authority, as the Nazis did, supposedly.

In the wake of these theories it has become widely accepted, with a curious mixture of horror and relish—especially among intellectuals—that potentially all of us are amoral, robotic monsters, but monsters without convictions, distinction or originality. There was something morbidly fascinating about the combination of extraordinary moral outrages (such as the Nazis perpetrated) and the pedestrian, mundane character of the perpetrators. The popularity of these ideas was nurtured by the questioning of modernity which brought us technology, mass production, efficiency, bureaucracy, impersonality, mass culture and the decline of community. These ideas were especially congenial with the protest movements of the 1960s whose stock in trade were impassioned critiques of impersonality, dehumanization and faceless bureaucracy.

The banality of evil approach also lent itself to a generous extension of the idea of "complicity" and the rejection of American (or any other Western) society. If anybody could readily become a mass murderer, or assist in mass murder, and if beliefs and motivation were largely irrelevant to behavior, then no society was immune to genocidal temptations. Moreover the allegedly homogenized mass societies overly reliant on technology such as the U.S. might have a special affinity to devising new, efficient forms of mass murder, even genocide. Not by accident did "genocide" and "genocidal" become favorite epithets of the social critics and political activists of the 1960s (hardly ever directed at truly genocidal political systems). It may also be recalled here that the 1960s generation of radicals took great pleasure in comparing the United States to Nazi Germany (they spelled America with a "k") and whenever possible threw at it terms like "fascist," and "nazi" and compared American institutions to the Gestapo, the storm troopers and Auschwitz.

The Vietnam War further stimulated the inclination to associate mass murder with technology and view the United States as a genocidal country intent on killing good-natured peasants impersonally with sophisticated technology from high altitudes, rather than in manly, authentic, face-to-face combat. American soldiers in this perspective were "professional killers" and their lack of passion was also held against them by many anti-war activists. Repeatedly such critics of the United States contrasted favorably the supposedly poorly armed, deeply committed, simple guerillas, operating in small groups with the mechanized might of the U.S. forces for whom fighting was a "job" to be performed impersonally and efficiently.

The recent waves of political violence committed by Islamic groups and individuals have dealt a heavy blow to the theories and ideas Arendt popularized. A greatly neglected factor of political conflict and violence suddenly and dramatically reemerged, namely, fanatical hatred and the religious-political beliefs generating it. It was these beliefs that legitimated the ruthless violence the hatred inspired. Rarely in history has the relationship between belief and behavior been so clear as in the actions of the Islamic suicide pilots and bombers fortified and reassured as they had been by conceptions and personifications of evil defined with great clarity and held unhesitatingly. There was nothing banal, impersonal, dispassionate or detached about their behavior. A pure, burning hatred of the evil eagerly embraced motivated them as well as certain specific, if peculiar but deeply felt beliefs in other-wordily rewards. (More down to earth motives also played a part as families receive substantial material compensation for their "martyred" sons or daughters in addition to a marked improvement of their social standing in the community which applauds suicide bombings.)

In numerous Arab countries and communities a hate-filled political culture evolved which enshrines violence as a sacred mission directed at the designated objects of hate. In these settings virulent hatred is inculcated from an early age; it is disseminated by the mass media, in schools and places of worship and sanctioned by both religious and political authorities.

It is one thing to kill or harm one's enemies in a matter-of-fact way in combat or in what is usually perceived as self-defense, and something quite different to publicly rejoice in, celebrate and glorify such killings. It is the hallmark of a political culture drenched in self-righteous hate that it allows and encourages individuals to joyously display their bloody hands to television cameras and bystanders after they committed murder, as was the case last year when two Israeli soldiers were lynched on the West Bank. The same political culture sustains the behavior of people who dance on the streets when hearing about the indiscriminate mass murder of their supposed enemies, as was the case in several Arab cities after September 11. One can also readily associate this political culture with the attitude of parents who express great joy upon hearing of the "martyrdom" their children incurred in the course of blowing to bits innocent civilians.

Whatever the ingredients or sources of such hatred—material deprivation, lack of education, frustration, resentment, sense of inferiority, the scapegoating impulse—it has become the dominant force fuelling political conflict and violence. Its "root cause" is not poverty but relative deprivation or frustrated expectations and the overpowering but comforting belief that others are responsible for one's misfortune. It is highly relevant here to recall that (as reported in a recent New York Times op-ed piece) opinion polls in the West Bank and Gaza found "that better educated Palestinians were more likely than others to approve of violence."

There is certainly nothing banal or inauthentic about the violence of the suicide bombers enthusiastically killing themselves in the pursuit of their ideals. Religious beliefs and a climate of public opinion legitimate and nurture such hatreds, which in other cultures most people are embarrassed to display in public, let alone act on.

It is perhaps the authenticity of such violence and the belief that its perpetrators are the virtuous victims of the West (of the United States, and Israel) that impels the hardcore supporters of the adversary culture in this country to take a more charitable view of it and its perpetrators. Even if these warriors have not attracted as much open sympathy as the Vietcong used to, they benefit from the identity of their enemies in the eyes of the radical-left beholders whose better known representatives include Noam Chomsky, Terry Eagelton, Barbara Ehrenreich, Eric Foner, Frederic Jameson, Norman Mailer, Katha Pollit, Edward Said, Susan Sontag and Gore Vidal, among many others. They cannot help being drawn to virtually any group or individual passionately opposed to and willing to take militant action against the United States and Israel since they regard the United States "the great Satan" and the source of all evil and injustice in this world and Israel its ally and lackey.

In the wake of 9/11 these attitudes have taken several forms. One was the search for "root causes" which invariably led to the conclusion that the United States and Israel are in the final analysis responsible for the violence directed against them; if they are so bitterly hated there have to be good reasons for such hate. Another expression of the same attitude was the solicitousness shown toward those accused of or suspected of the terrorist violence against the U.S. and Israel. A great surge of concern about their civil and human rights and welfare swept through left-liberal circles that would be praiseworthy if such concern had also been shown for the corresponding rights and welfare of the victims of the various anti-Western, anti-American and anti-Israeli gueril/as and movements.

At numerous universities administrators have been anxious to protect the sensitivity of Arab students and adherents of Islamic beliefs by deeming offensive any expression of American patriotism including the display of the American flag; likewise campus critics of the U.S. war on terrorism in Afghanistan and elsewhere were assured a far more supportive environment than those supporting it.

Another symbolic gesture of support and solidarity was extended by Western "peace activists" who rushed to Arafat's headquarters in Ramallah and to the besieged terrorists in the Church of Nativity in Bethlehem to keep them company and protect them by their presence.

There have also been many attempts to deny that Islamic religious beliefs could have inspired or legitimated the murderous political impulses and behavior of the suicide bombers. These attempts are reminiscent of the old dispute about the relationship between Marxism and the practices of communist states. The repressive nature of these states cannot be directly blamed on Marx and his theories but there was a connection, at the very least in the sense of entitlement to ruthlessness on behalf of great ideals to be realized. A paradise awaiting the suicide bomber is such an ideal or aspiration, and it is a religious notion not invented by the individuals in question who act on it. None of the other violent enemies of Western societies in recent times (the Weathermen, the Red Brigade in Italy, the Bader-Meinhof gang in Germany, the IRA in Ireland, the Basque terrorists etc) were suicidal. They did not have the kind of religious assurance and encouragement their Islamic counterparts possess at the present time.

The evil of Nazism was not banal, nor is the evil of Islamic suicide bombers. Whatever the social and political circumstances which contribute to their actions they do not provide moral license or the kind of "understanding" that shades into a mitigation of their behavior; these were individuals who, according to all indications, choose their actions freely, with utmost deliberation and under no compulsion other than the prodding of their beliefs and the enthusiastic support of their community.

Paul Hollander is professor emeritus of sociology at the University of Massachusetts, Amherst. His books include *Political Pilgrims, Anti-Americanism, Political Will and Personal Belief* and most recently *Discontents: Postmodern and Postcommunist* (Transaction, 2002).

NOTES

1. This holds true despite the fact that the ex-Communist countries which have recently adopted democracy and privatization, most notably Russia, are experiencing immense difficulties in adopting the Western model. It must be borne in mind that even the Communist parties of these countries no longer talk of a return to the Soviet model. They want to blend democracy and the market with social-welfare policies and a certain degree of government intervention in the economy—not an infeasible combination.

2. The fictitious contrast between the "rights of property" and the "rights of men" was drawn as early as 1910 by Theodore Roosevelt and restated by Franklin Delano Roosevelt in 1936. See Tom Bethell, The Noblest Triumph, which I reviewed in the November 1998 Commentary.

3. This Hegelian-Marxist group-based morality, of course challenges the central tenets of the Judeo-Christian and Kantian Enlightenment ethical framework—loosely put, that individuals are responsible for their own actions, and that humans should be treated as "ends" in themselves and not as simply "means" to an "end" (such as the creation of a new and better society).

4. Interestingly, Gramsci himself understood that America was exceptional. He noted that the Protestant ethic was more universally assimilated by the "popular masses" in America than anywhere else because of the absence of what he called "parasitic classes" (i.e. aristocratic, clerical) that have been central to "European civilization." Gramsci labeled this exceptionalism "Americanism" or "Fordism" and astutely recognized that the task of achieving socialism would be much tougher in America than in Europe.

5. Joseph A. Schumpeter, *Capitalism, Socialism and Democracy* (New York: Harper and Row, 1947), pp. 147–148.

6. Ibid.

7. Eric Hoffer, *First things, Last Things* (New York: Harper and Row, 1971), p. 85.

8. Thomas Sowell, *The Vision of the Anointed* (New York: Basic Books, 1995).

Further Reading

Bernstein, Richard. *Dictatorship of Virtue: Multiculturalism and the Battle for America's Future.* New York: Alfred A. Knopf, 1994.

Bunzel, John H., ed. *Political Passages: Journeys of Change Through Two Decades, 1968–1988.* New York: The Free Press, 1988.

Hanson, Victor Davis, John Heath, and Bruce S. Thornton. *Bonfire of the Humanities: Rescuing the Classics in an Impoverished Age.* Wilmington, DE: ISI Books, 2001.

Hollander, Paul. *Political Pilgrims: Travels of Western Intellectuals to the Soviet Union, China, and Cuba, 1928–1978.* New York: Oxford, 1981.

Horowitz, David. *The Politics of Bad Faith: The Radical Assault on America's Future.* New York: Touchstone, 1998.

Hunter, James Davison. *Culture Wars: The Struggle to Define America.* New York: BasicBooks, 1991.

Kors, Alan Charles, and Harvey A. Silvergate. *The Shadow University.* New York: The Free Press, 1998.

Simon, Julian. *The Ultimate Resource.* Princeton, NJ: Princeton University Press, 1981.

Sommers, Christina Hoff. *Who Stole Feminism? How Women Have Betrayed Women.* New York: Touchstone, 1994.

Index

About the Author

GEORGE ZILBERGELD is Associate Professor and Chair of the Political Science Department at Montclair State University.